Men of my Father's Generation

Lessons of Courage, Christianity and Conscience from a Generation Removed from Slavery

James W. Thornton

Men of My Father's Generation

Copyright © 2014 by James W. Thornton

ISBN: 978-0-9839483-5-3

Library of Congress Number 2014947940

All Rights Reserved. No part of this publication may be reproduced, stored in a retrieval system, or transmitted in any way by any means—electronic, mechanical, photocopy, recording, or otherwise, without the prior permission of the copyright holder, except as provided by USA copyright law.

Scriptures taken from the NEW AMERICAN STANDARD BIBLE®, Copyright © 1960,1962,1963,1968,1971,1972,1973,1975,1977,1995 by The Lockman Foundation. All rights reserved.

Scriptures taken from the HOLY BIBLE, NEW INTERNATIONAL VERSION ®. Copyright © 1973, 1978, 1984 Biblical. Used by permission of Zondervan. All rights reserved.

Scripture quotations marked "[NLT]" are taken from the Holy Bible, New Living Translation, copyright © 1996, 2004, 2007. Used by permission of Tyndale House Publishers, Inc., Carol Stream, Illinois 60188. All rights reserved.

Scripture quotations marked "[AMP]" are taken from The Amplified Bible, Old Testament copyright ®1965, 1987 by the Zondervan Corporation and The Amplified New Testament copyright ® 1958, 1987 by The Lockman Foundation. Used by permission. Printed in the United States of America. First Edition 2011. All rights reserved.

Greek definitions retrieved from *A Greek-English Lexicon*, Ninth Edition. Copyright © 1996 Clarendon Foundation - Oxford. All rights reserved.

Acknowledgements and Thanks

To my father, Oscar Thornton. My dad was the most incredible man I have ever known. His life was a true depiction of Christ. He lived as God commanded, not with words, but with his actions. Everywhere he went, and everyone he met, he made a difference. His legacy continues to live within our hearts, and will do so, even when we are gone. I thank God for putting such a man in my life.

The encounter my father had with the Lord at a young age forever changed him to such a degree that he made it his mission to impact others in a positive way. He provided for those that were sick in the community, as well as the widows. He lived the scriptures in Acts 20:35.

To my mother, Bernice Thornton. A wife, mother, and grandmother who instilled in me, along with my dad, values, morals, and the love of Christ. Thanks mom for the great stories and memories about dad.

To my wife Nathalee. Thank you for giving me the support, encouragement, love and prayers that was needed throughout the years

To my children, Cynthia, Austell, Mechelle, and James; and my son-in-law Johnny Ray Pruitt. Thank you for your prayers, support, and encouragement.

To my church family and the many friends who I couldn't mention for that would be a book within itself. Thank you all for your prayers, support and encouragement.

Dedication

Men of my Father's Generation, is a tribute to individuals who chose to take responsibility despite their obstacles. These individuals were one generation removed from slavery. This special group of people consisted of former slaves, and grandsons of former slave owners. They were driven by a desire and purpose to take a righteous cause and go against the grain, making a difference in their generation. Both former slaves and grandsons of former slave owners made a decision and placed a demand on themselves to rise above the circumstance and the position of the majority. While many former slaves knew very little about responsibility, these men took on the responsibility of being husbands, fathers, providers, protectors, and teachers. This level of knowledge did not come from their history, but from the Source that made them.

Foreword

The book you are now reading presents an opportunity for us to reflect on an important journey that took place largely in the preceding generation, and chronicles the enduring impact of relationships that men, and their families had on each other during that period. The book gives an enriching look at those relationships that could, and in reality, did exist, during an important time in our history when some realized that we are the *"Same Kind of Different..."* (From the powerful book written by Denver Moore and Ron Hall entitled "Some Kind of Different as Me"). **"Men of My Father's Generation"** represents some of those who saw and reflected on differences that did exist among men and their families, but further, the likenesses that were present when people lost those differences and placed into practice the attributes of Christian caring, love, and support.

I arrived in the community as a teenager and was blessed to meet and know some of the men of Dr. Thornton's father's generation, and I am a better person from having done so. A deep appreciation was gained when a person witnessed the true caring of those individuals, along with relationships that bridged the generation. Of course, the author recognized that relationships with all people were not always so positive.

I will always treasure the kind and caring friendship that I developed with Oscar, Dr. Thornton's father. He was truly a gentle man of great insight and caring. I recall Oscar, along with several men from the Post Oak Methodist Church were working on a special project of completing the landscaping related to the final stages of construction of the church and parsonage. Oscar took great pride in his work, and also, great pride in encouraging others to grow and develop. As he planted a shrub outside the church, approximately even with the church altar, Oscar proclaimed, "I am naming this shrub BISHOP. Watch it grow." As he made that pronouncement, he looked quietly at me with a huge smile, which was his trademark, and nodded his head in a positive way. He was sending a clear message of confidence in me that I would continue to grow as well. Oscar's impact on me and my family continues to this day.

I salute the author for his work as he chronicled the relationships. As well, you are certain to appreciate the journey written by my friend, Dr. James Thornton – **"Men of My Father's Generation."**

Dr. Nathan Hodges
College President, Retired

Table of Contents

Introduction: A Profile of Courage..................................xiii

Chapter One..19
    Special Men of My Father's Generation

Chapter Two..27
    The Education of My Father's Generation

Chapter Three..37
Salvation in My Father's Generation

Chapter Four...49
    Grace in My Father's Generation

Chapter Five...57
    God's Strength Through Prayer in My Father's Generation

Chapter Six..63
    Identity Crisis of the Church and Man in My Father's Generation

Chapter Seven..73
    Finding True Identity Brings Humility in My Father's Generation

Chapter Eight..87
    Acknowledging the Father in My Father's Generation

Chapter Nine...97
    The Beginning of Physical Change in My Father's Generation

Chapter Ten...103

Freedom in My Father's Generation

Chapter Eleven 113
    Moving Forward in My Father's Generation

Chapter Twelve 123
    The Hope of My Father's Generation for the Next Generation

Final Thoughts **133**

Introduction:
A Profile of Courage

The time was in the year of our Lord, 1932, when a young black kid left home after having a dispute with his stepfather. The story goes on to say that this one particular Caucasian family that knew him from birth made provisions for him to stay in one of their homes. The head of the Caucasian family was a man whom everyone called "Daddy Jim," an educator and a farmer, who later became the County Tax Assessor. The young black kid was my father, Oscar Thornton.

There are things about the relationship between my father and Jim Jernigan's family, as well as his own family that my father never revealed. For instance, my father shared little about his natural father with his children, although he did say his stepmother, Estella Petty, his father's wife treated him as her biological son. However, my knowledge of the relationship that he had with the Jernigan family from my earliest childhood years stands out as not being the norm, especially from the part of the nation where we lived. We lived in the southeast part of the state of Alabama – a state known for its racism, bigotry and its allegiance to the *"Old South."* The environment in which we lived in the 1940s, '50s and '60s was often depicted in movies and newspapers as a harsh and poverty-stricken environment for people of color. We must remember that this state has its place in history. Montgomery was the capital of the Confederacy, as well as the birthplace of the Civil Rights movement. You can see how living on the land owned by the Jernigan family can be best described as living in the South; however, our living arrangement was not influenced by the ways of the South. It was as if we were living in an environment that was free from the environment that controlled the rest of the South. In other words, we lived in a southern state, but the environment of that state didn't live in us.

Now, I was aware of the traditional South when my parents would take me to town. I saw everything was segregated. I witnessed when the merchants would service the whites first, and then they would serve the "colored" using the term "boy" when they were addressing individuals who were in the same ethnic group as we were. I would hear stories of how other blacks were being treated, and that at the homes of many whites, the blacks had to come in through the back door. This was not the case with my family. While we lived on the land owned by the Jernigan family. We came into whatever door we wanted to, and they called us by our given name or a nickname. We ate at the same table at the same time.

My mother, who just celebrated her 89th birthday, shares many stories on the relationship with the Jernigans. She has frequently stated that her relationship with "Mama Lenora" exceeded that of her own mother. She told us of many occasions where Mama Nora (short for Lenora) would access our house while we were at the Macedonia Baptist Church, bringing dinner to feed an army and leave it on the table. My father was one of the young deacons at the church, and he would always invite a large percentage of the church to come to our house for lunch. My mother asked Mama Nora why she would bring extra food, and her explanation was, "I know my son Oscar, and he has such a good heart." Yes, this woman called my father her son, and would introduce my sisters and brothers, as well as me as her grandchildren. This was an incredible family.

The Jernigan family owned two stores in the community, of which one of the stores my father managed. From the time I was in the tenth grade until the year I finished high school, my dad ran their family's country store. My dad kept the records of the purchased goods, and he ordered all the supplies. This particular store was the gathering place for both whites and blacks. While many that came to the store shared their deep-rooted negative views of whites and blacks, they never voiced their negative views in the store. This story was told to me by the daughter-in law of Daddy Jim, a person that I call to this day Aunt Lou. She stated that an old black man that everybody called Uncle Whit was present when one of the white men said there would be two heavens and two bodies. Uncle Whit was bold enough to say to the man, "Mister, there is only one heaven, and it is available to all who accept the Lord Jesus Christ." Unfortunately, this concept shared by the white man was not uncommon. However, the fact that Uncle Whit was bold enough to say what he said spoke volumes of the confidence that he had in the leadership of Daddy Jim. Uncle Whit knew that he could express his heart without there being a consequence.

Two of the many talents of my father were cleaning out existing wells full of water, and digging wells for water. Like any mother concerned for her son, Mama Nora was very upset every time he went into a well. She expressed her displeasure to such a degree that he finally stopped. Daddy Jim placed my father in a leadership role on the farm and in other endeavors. They wanted him to succeed in all aspects of his life. His leadership role on the farm was such that whatever he said was the final decision. In that era, such decisions were typically made by the owners of farms and not the black farmers, but this was the only environment that we knew.

As a child, I observed the love and the courage of my father and the Jernigan family, but I didn't fully understand the significance of it until I was a private in the Army in 1961 when I was stationed in Germany. I was informed by a fellow soldier that I had received a telephone call. To my surprise, it was from Colonel Lynn Jernigan, the older son of the Jernigan family. He invited me - a private - to his home for Christmas dinner. Although I didn't go, it had a lasting effect on me. I remember as a child, Uncle PJ, one of Daddy Jim's sons, taught me the radio Morse code, whereby I could communicate with people as far away as Hawaii. My relationship with him exceeded the relationship I had with my biological uncles.

The loving traits of this family were passed on to their children, as well as their grandchildren. During a recent meeting with Daddy Jim's granddaughter, she informed me that she always saw us as part of their family. She didn't see black or white; she saw family. This family displayed the teaching of the Lord Jesus Christ.

In the Jernigan home, we experienced a time of unprecedented calmness even though there were laws promulgated by man that sought to restrict and place everyone in a form of bondage. I came to learn that the Jernigan family demonstrated the love of the Lord in treating us with dignity. Their love was unconditional. They could have taken the same path as many because they lived in a state that had demonstrated its hatred for individuals of our ethnicity. No one is perfect, but the Jernigans demonstrated a kind of love that was above, and from above. The "n" word was used by Mama Nora, but my father and mother immediately would express their displeasure, and she knew it. As we grew older, the "n" word was no longer in her vocabulary.

The humble families that influenced my father's generation allowed the teaching of the Lord Jesus to shape their views and gave my father great courage in living an integrated life and pushing for integration for everyone. This courage was demonstrated for all to see, and it was obvious that many whites in the community didn't mirror the same conviction. However, the men of my father's generation that wanted to see widespread change in how they were treated remained steadfast.

Despite the changes that have occurred over that last fifty years, the time I spent with the Jernigan family was a great and special time for me. We understood the natural limitation, but the spiritual truth constantly remained. A lack of knowledge existed then; and, it seems as if that same lack of knowledge has intensified today. I recently saw a teacher of mine who is now in her eighties. She expressed a disappointment of the current status quo. She said, "It is if we went out of light into a world of darkness and confusion. The new laws of man can never replace the teaching of the Lord Jesus."

Modernization has given man huge advantages. Innovations have changed the perspective, and laws promulgated by man have elevated his status, shaped his vision, and placed great emphasis on his achievements. The irony of this was while man has landed on the moon, men on earth in this country cannot live together in peace. The men of my father's generation recognized that the condition of their heart ranked higher spiritually than what they achieved in the natural. Hard work and providing for one's family was the order of the day. They understood the value of responsibility, the ability to respond. Welfare and government handouts were taboo; these men took pleasure in accepting their responsibility.

Even in the midst of their horrific conditions these men of my Father's generation stand out as unique individuals who made a positive impact on their community, state, and the nation. They refused to be denied; they focused on a greater power than the government. They placed relationship above religion, tradition, and the laws of man. Neither religion, tradition nor the laws of man can replace truth and righteousness. They refused to allow the circumstances to establish their true identity.

I remember a fishing trip Uncle PJ persuaded me to go on with my father and James Meredith, who was seeking to integrate "Ole Miss." At no point did Uncle PJ express opposition to Mr. Meredith getting a decent education, and I believe Uncle PJ knew that as some point integration would have to take place based on laws that were being implemented. (True integration, however, would not come through the laws of man, but by the teaching of the Lord Jesus Christ.) The men of my father's generation knew that the cycle had to be broken. My father was instrumental in bringing this together. His knowledge of the Word made him aware of the condition of the status quo and the need to pull down the stronghold that existed, even in the church. These men knew that truth would come under attack, but the truth would prevail.

Today, as I look back, I see great and courageous men, both black and white. They lived in a time when no one locked their doors, a time when a community expressed the love of the Lord by sharing with one another. These men played a vital role in "standing in the gap" for the nation. While the elite made positive impacts in the national development of the nation, these men made positive impacts in praying for the nation. They represented Jesus, not with words, but with action. (2 Chronicles 7:14).

Chapter One
Special Men of My Father's Generation

While it is obvious that little or no preparation was provided for the former slaves as it relates to adjusting to the new position of freedom, many revealed a trait of leadership that could only come from the Source that created them. This source of wisdom was from God. Their lack of knowledge was compensated by the Holy Spirit, who guided them into a truth of which they were not aware. Remember, they were one generation removed from slavery, and this generation was suffering from the residual effects of slavery. These effects consisted of poverty, lack of work, lack of knowledge, adjusting to this new life of freedom, and an education system that did not provide for the ex-slaves. Sadly, one of the most powerful effects of slavery was a lack of spiritual truth.

A lack of knowledge concerning the Word was one of the means of keeping the slaves in check. This new founded freedom did very little to remove this deficiency. The slaves received conflicting points of view to keep them in check; the slaves were told their condition was ordained of God. Hence, if it is ordained of God, why fight it? This attitude remained as powerful after slavery as during slavery. "Jim Crow" exercised its authority with impunity. So while the ex-slaves were free legally, they were mentally and spiritually still in bondage. However, since God makes known the end from the beginning, He had a plan to deal with this manner.

As these men grew in their relationship with the Lord Jesus, the Holy Spirit began to guide them into a truth that passed all natural understanding. John 16:13 says, "But when He, the Spirit of Truth (the Truth-giving Spirit) comes, He will guide you into all the Truth (the whole, full Truth). For He will not speak His own message [on His own authority]; but He will tell whatever He hears [from the Father; He will give the message that has been given to Him], and He will announce and declare to you the things that are to come [that will happen in the future]," (AMP). It was the pouring out of the Holy Spirit that influenced these men of my father's generation. These men played greater value on the finished work of the Lord Jesus, than on the laws of man. They saw each challenge as an opportunity.

Not fully comprehending the principles of God did not prevent them from being driven. The knowledge they had was sufficient. The Holy Spirit drove them in the same manner as when the Son was led into the wilderness by the Holy Spirit in Mark. 1:12, "Immediately the Spirit impelled Him *to go* out in the wilderness," (NAS). It was in the wilderness that the Son of Man discovered Who He was. In Luke 4:17-21, it says, "And the book of the Prophet Isaiah was handed to Him, And He opened the book and found the place where it was written, 'The Spirit of the Lord is upon Me, Because He anointed Me to Preach the gospel to the poor. He has sent Me to proclaim release to the captives, And recovery of sight to the blind, to set free those who are oppressed, to proclaim The favorable year of the Lord. And He closed the book, and gave it back to the Attendant and sat down; and the eyes of all in the synagogue were fixed on Him. And He began to say to them, Today this Scripture has been fulfilled in your hearing," (NAS). Knowledge of this truth motivated the former slaves to seek understanding, and many sons of former slave owners provided this understanding. They suddenly realized the information they were given by their fathers was in violation of the principles of God. They realized that out of one blood, He made all nations.

While the founders and their fathers were driven by a "law" mentality, these men tapped into truth concerning race. Salvation is not about the works of the product, but by the Grace of God, the

… Father through His Son Jesus Christ. Grace and Truth are partners. Truth exposed the condition of every creature; all have missed the mark. No one group was superior to another, and no one group was inferior to another. Salvation and equality were established by God when He created the product in His image and after His likeness. The product, being inferior to the knowledge of God could never on his own come up with a way to please Him. These individuals recognized the predicament they were in and that the only means of going forward was through Jesus Christ.

Strength Despite Challenge

The men of my father's generation were special men of courage, strength, boldness and dedication. Men who sought themselves based on the Word of God and not on the words of mere men. These men refused to take the path of least resistance and refused to allow their circumstances to identify them. These men sought to learn and develop the traits of integrity, accountability, discipline, and responsibility. They placed others above themselves, *and* looked not at the things that were seen. 2 Corinthians 4:18 says, "Since we consider and look not to the things that are seen but to the things that are unseen; for the things that are visible are temporal (brief and fleeting), but the things that are invisible are deathless and everlasting," (AMP). The seen world produced hopelessness, bondage, fear, intimidation, and a slave mentality.

These men chose to allow the Word to identify them. The Word took a higher place of honor than the old ways of slavery and second-class citizenship. The old way that consisted of exploitation and an abusive environment produced an attitude whereby they were seen as less than human. To bring creditability to this lie, a segment of the church [the source of light] embraced this teaching. This teaching defined democracy as a system of government ordained by God; therefore, it was God's will that these special men comply with the current order of things. This was another example of men embracing the kingdom of this world as if it were the kingdom of heaven. In a system where darkness was seen as light, a lie took precedence over truth, and death was seen as life. These men looked beyond the natural. Their focus was on the Word. The fact that many had little or no education did not deter my father and the special men of his generation from accepting responsibility. Despite living in such a hostile environment, they refused to give up, give out, or give in to the pressure. They maintained a resilient spirit. Even when their country rejected and spoke evil of them, making derogatory remarks, these derogatory remarks were not their reality. These men were intuitively moved to believe that God had a plan for their lives. Jeremiah 29:11 says, "For I know the thoughts and plans that I have for you, says the Lord, thoughts and plans for welfare and peace and not for evil, to give you hope I your final outcome," (AMP). Obviously, the founders and the leaders of their generation did not know that the Creator of the Universe (God) had a plan for all lives in the earth, including ex-slaves. The negative attitudes of the founders and leaders did not prevent these men from being dedicated and willing to protect the so called "land of the free, and home of the brave." The founders and movers of their day made a mockery out of the truth by confessing their Christianity, but refusing to honor their own words.

The refusal to enforce the existing laws was evident that man without divine intervention was helpless. Pride became a stronghold; therefore, the focus was on the founders and not on the Creator. The founders and leaders of my father's generation refused to be men of integrity; they refused to enforce the 13th, 14th, and 15th amendments to the Constitution. Yet, these men maintained their dedication to their country despite the country's attitude toward them. Those who went into the military knew the responsibility that they would have to shoulder, putting their lives on the line

Men of My Father's Generation

to protect others abroad while being in legal bondage at home. They fought to protect citizens of other countries while they were refused their own rights. I remember my uncle, Louis, telling me that he was encouraged to join the Army by one of the local leaders. He was told that as an American, he had an obligation to protect his country. His response to the local leader was, "If I get killed, there is no place for me to be buried." However, despite these conditions, he gladly served his country with the greatest amount of honor, even though he was not allowed to vote in his own country.

The courage of these men was above reproach. Their conviction drove them to look beyond their present conditions. They had an unshakable belief that though they were abused, the Father of all fathers would vindicate them. In Hebrews 6:10, it says, "For God is not unrighteous to forget *or* overlook your labor and the love which you have shown for His name's sake in ministering to the needs of the saints (His own consecrated peoples), as you still do," (AMP). As it has been stated earlier, these men knew that those oppressing them were also oppressed. Thus, they continued to show respect to those that oppressed them, submitting to the status quo by walking in love. This level of love is revealed by the writer Paul in 1 Corinthians 13: 4, 6-7: "Love endures long, *and* is patient and kind; love never is envious *nor* boils over with jealousy, is not boastful *or* vainglorious, does not display itself haughtily. It does not rejoice at injustice and unrighteousness, but rejoices when right *and* truth prevail. Love bears up under anything and everything that comes, is ever ready to believe the best of every person, its hopes are fadeless under all circumstances, and it endures everything [without weakening]," (AMP). This process required a great commitment that the Father of light gave them. The process required a commitment that was released as a result of His grace. His grace considered the flaws of all, the oppressed and the oppressors, for all have missed the mark. No ethnic group is above reproach, and no ethnic group has a corner on truth. Grace and Truth came by Jesus Christ.

The special men of my father's generation were not contending against flesh and blood in overcoming their predicament. Ephesians 6:12 says, "For we are not wrestling with flesh and blood [contending only with physical opponents], but against the despotisms, against the powers, against [the master spirits who are] the world rulers of this present darkness, against the spirit forces of wickedness in the heavenly (supernatural) sphere," (AMP). This explains why the founders and the leaders of my father's generation could not see the evil that they were guilty of doing. These principalities, powers, and rulers of the darkness of this world blinded their eyes, and they could not see the depth of this evil. As a matter of fact, the oppressors were as blinded as the oppressed; both sides were the victim of the power of darkness.

The Voice Crying from the Ground

The voice of my father and the special men of his generation speak from the ground as Abel's blood cried out: "Tell our story, and tell it well." The story that must be told is: how courageous they were in taking a righteous stand (Joshua 1:7). The story consists of providing for the family in the midst of great challenges. The story consists of taking full responsibility in mentoring your children because the mentorship is for the present, as well as future generations. Each child born in the world comes with potential, purpose, and destiny, and fathers have the awesome responsibility of recognizing these traits and motivating their children. The voice that cries from the ground says the present situation of fathers abandoning their children is worse than slavery. The voices state very firmly that abandonment is an evil spirit that must be addressed by the church as well as the fathers.

Men of My Father's Generation

Government does not have the ability or the mandate that fathers have to provide for their children. The government can provide finance, but leadership is a requirement of the fathers. Abandonment produces wounds that can only be healed by a personal relationship with the Lord Jesus. Government cannot bring this healing. Government has failed in that those in positions of authority refused to enforce the laws promulgated by the founders. The 13th, 14th, and 15th Amendments were added to the Constitution long ago, but they were not fully executed, thus, the residual effect of slavery remains steadfast today. Remember, slavery is a product of an evil spirit because out of one blood, He made all ethnic groups. Acts 17:26 says, "And He made from one [common origin, one source, one blood} all nations of men to settle on the face of the earth...," (AMP). This means the same blood that redeemed the oppressor - the slave owner - also redeemed the slave - the oppressed; thus, no nation or ethnic group has a corner on righteousness or truth. To believe anything more was an indictment on the nation as well as the church. Both sides were confessing one thing with their mouth, but their action expressed an opposing view. First, the Father God is no respecter of person; He does not choose to release His glory on a particular group of individuals based on their ethnicity, nor is leadership based on one's ethnicity. This is the lie that the founders – as well as an aspect of the church – expressed. Color was not a factor.

God's grace and truth are not based on the color of one's skin. The product is a spirit made in the image and likeness of the Father, Son, and the Holy Spirit. The pouring of His spirit was upon all flesh. The criterion is the Lord Jesus Christ. Notice, the Bible does not say that salvation is the result of your ethnicity. It does not say that freedom is only available to those of a certain color. Romans 10:13 says, "For everyone who calls upon the name the Lord [invoking Him as Lord will be saved," (AMP). In John 8:36, it says, "So if the Son liberate you [makes you free men], then you are really and unquestionably free" (AMP). The action of the founders and an aspect of the church go against these scriptures. The men of my father's generation had to overcome these obstacles and be the men whom they were created to be. They could not place confidence in the system of government or an aspect of the church because an aspect of the church and the leaders of the nation worked in unison to protect the lie and prevent the ethnic group that these men represented from achieving.

The men of my father's generation were special men for the mere fact, they understood the Source and his Word, and lived by both.

Chapter Two
The Education of My Father's Generation

Education was something that was extremely valuable to the men of my father's generation. A fifth grade education was comparable to a high school education today. To these individuals, education was not only about the ABCs- reading, writing and arithmetic. It was also about a life focused on the finished work of Jesus Christ.

The men of my father's generation were born in the nineteen-twenties. They were one generation removed from slavery. They had to deal with many issues that were not experienced by the founders. While the founders sought to establish this country on principles that went beyond the caste system, they without knowing kept that same door open. That door elevated the status of one ethnic group over another, and expanded the boundaries of the caste system to include race, as if individuals had anything to do with the ethnicity that they were assigned. They failed to comprehend that all ethnic groups were created in His image and after His likeness.

The same lack of knowledge that released the caste system in Europe played its hand in this nation. Thus, the Europeans as well as founders of this nation faced the same enemy, and they were duped because of a lack of knowledge. This lack of knowledge has blinded generation after generation from the truth. The writer in Proverbs 14: 12 expressed it well: "There is a way that seemeth right to a man, but the end thereof are the ways of death," (KJV). This profound statement of truth is evident today as the nation continues to wander off the path of righteousness. While today the division is equal to that of the Civil War, the men of my father's generation had to face this challenge, and made the decision to rise above it. They didn't have access to education or modern technology; they had access to the Word. The Word that they knew brought them great reward, wisdom, knowledge and understanding. Even to those that could not read, the Holy Spirit reminded them of the finished work of the Lord Jesus. His work was complete, and since they were in Him; what they lacked, the Holy Spirit would provide.

The Holy Spirit made His provisions available to the descendants of former slaves as well as the descendants of former slave owners. The availability was to them that believed. This group of men united together in the same manner as the saints of old: the abolitionists in taking a stand for right, justice, and equality. They were a powerful source in the remaking of a nation. While the devastation of the Civil War left wounds like no other war in American history, these men saw opportunity where others saw obstacles. Many of the descendants of slavery could only see obstacles. They were ill-prepared for a transition from slavery to freedom. The freedom that they were promised had not manifested; the concept, "Land of the free and home of the brave" was not their reality. The concept, "One nation under God," brought confusion and brought the questions, "Would a Holy God allow this to happen?" or "Would a Holy God that created one is His image de-value them to be servants to others? Being servants to others is the greatest example of aborting potential and purpose.

The confusion intensified when it was known that the former slaves were considered less in value than others. The confusion rose to the level of resentment and hatred: resentment and hatred toward the Heavenly Father, the former slave owners, and the carpetbaggers who continued to exploit them. Obviously, their resentment for the Father was the result of a lack of knowledge on their part, because God is holy, and His word does not change. His ways are higher than the highest way of the product. Isaiah 55:8-9 says, "For My thoughts are not your thoughts, neither are your ways My ways, says the Lord. For as the heavens are higher than the earth, so are My ways higher than your ways and My thoughts than your thoughts," (AMP). Herein lies the great disconnect; His thoughts are so superior to the product as light is superior to dark and life is superior to being dead.

Nevertheless, many descendants of slavery blamed God for their situation. The former slave owners planted this seed, and the harvest of that seed is still seen today. One cannot add to God's Word or take away from His Word and maintain the relationship. The men of my father's generation lived in an environment whereby the source of light the church was more influenced by the world than the Lord Jesus. It is safe to say that they had zeal for God, but the zeal was not according to knowledge. This concept was not a new phenomenon. Paul wrote about this in Romans 10:2-3, "I bear them witness that they have a [certain] zeal *and* enthusiasm for God, but it is not enlightened *and* according to [correct and vital] knowledge. For being ignorant of the righteousness that God ascribed [which makes one acceptable to Him in word, thought, and deed] and seeking to establish a *righteousness* (a means of salvation) of their own, they did not obey *or* submit themselves to God's righteousness," (AMP). In their eyes, they could reconnect to God by adhering to their way. In other words, they could reconnect to God as a result of religion. This lack of knowledge removed the importance of the Lord Jesus Christ.

The combination of post-Civil War, a lack of knowledge and a hardened heart left the country in a state of chaos. To add fuel to the fire, there was a lack of leadership on the part of a segment of the church. This segment of the church not only supported the status quo but advocated it as "Godly inspired." The courageous men, then, had to depend on a source greater than man, greater than the best intention of the best agent of the government. In this hostile environment, the leading of the Holy Spirit was essential if they were to overcome the challenges that faced them. They didn't have the benefit of some government department watching over them, nor did they have the church standing in the gap for them. They had to learn to trust and obey based on the knowledge that they processed. The Spirit of Truth gave them the ability and the desire to set their affection on things above. These men were men without a nation, without rights and privileges that were available to others, even though their allegiance to this nation was above reproach. They served their country well by fighting on its behalf when democracy and freedom were threatened. The Spirit of Truth and the grace of the Lord Jesus gave them the ability and willingness to take godly responsibility in providing for their families as well as those in the community that were fatherless. It was not the norm for a child to grow up without a male mentor. Whether it was the grandfather, uncle, or a deacon in the church, the men of my father's generation took on that responsibility. In the natural, it was an impossible task.

While the nation had been poisoned by those that wanted things to remain as they were, little or no preparation was provided for the descendants of slaves to enter the mainstream of society. Much emphasis was placed on the lie that they were inferior. This lie continues to rear its ugly head in every aspect of our lives as a man, a husband, father, and a citizen of a nation that advocates her allegiance to the Lord Jesus Christ. Remember His words in John 13:34-35: "I give you a new commandment: that you should love one another. Just as I have loved you, so you too should love one another. By this shall all [men] know that you are My disciples, if you have love for one another [if you keep on showing love among yourselves,"] (AMP). Remember, this was not something that He suggested. It was a command! The command was to love one another "Just as I have loved you." Romans 5:8 tells us that

Men of My Father's Generation

He loved us while we (all mankind) were sinning: "But God shows *and* clearly proves His [own] love for us by the fact that while we were sinners, Christ (the Messiah, the anointing One) died for us" (AMP). The "us" consists of all ethnic groups that believe, therefore, no one ethnic group has a corner on truth.

There was a significant level of love that carried the men of my father's generation through many challenges where they continued loving those that hated them, loving those that abused them, and loving those that exploited them. Love that said one thing on Sunday in church, but chose to do the opposite Monday morning through Saturday in the cotton field, the sawmills, and even in the military. This kind of love enabled them to share their resources with others, including those of another ethnic group. I remember a story Mr. Paul shared with me about my father giving his resources to help a Caucasian family that was in need. While everyone showed their appreciation, the father of the Caucasian family was heard saying, "No nigger will give me anything." Another example of God's love was shown by the Jernigan family. Daddy Jim's love for my father changed my father's perspective of love for all mankind. A person of another ethnicity showing my father the love of the Lord that is found in John 13:35, and 1 John 4:20 was motivated by his love for Jesus Christ.

The Jernigans displayed love in many facets. They encouraged getting an education, voting and exercising their voting rights. One of the measuring stick of Daddy Jim's love was demonstrated in his willingness to teach my father and others how to read and write. He played a significant role in persuading an Alabama county to change the bus route so that the black children had access to it. On the days it would rain and the bus driver was not able pick us up because of the dirt road, a member of the Jernigan family would arrange for us to get to and from school. Their love was not limited to one generation; it was transferable to include their sons-in-law and daughters-in-law. The sons and sons-in-law were the pall-bearers at my father's funeral. This love remained in place even today.

I had a recent conversation with the granddaughter of Mr. Jim. She informed me that when her father was out of work, my dad asked him if he needed anything, and when my dad was out of work, the family gave him money. This relationship didn't fit the image that one read in books or saw in movies or television. Obviously, this stereotype-casting has shaped how the nation and the world views relationship. I am not trying to demise or deny all the negative things that took place, but there were Caucasians that showed the love of Jesus Christ, such as the Jernigans. Mr. Collie, one of the older sons of Mr. and Mrs. Jim Jernigan, made sure that I had an opportunity to make money for my school activities by providing me work throughout the year, and the pay was very good. Evidence of their love for my family and me were transferable after my father died. Mr. PJ and his wife, Aunt Louise, would take my younger brothers on vacation with them. When they were playing football, Aunt Louise would come and pick them up. This family had the grace of the Lord Jesus Christ upon them in that their love was genuine.

The love of the Lord Jesus Christ was demonstrated in every aspect of their lives. My dad and Uncle PJ would share their hearts to another. One of his brothers told me that "Paul would tell Oscar (my father) what he would tell his brothers." Again, this relationship was as solid as a rock. Uncle PJ shared something with me when I was a young man. He said, "The southerners see blacks as individuals, the northerners as a group. Both sides have a challenge in accepting blacks as equal." The Jernigan family saw the challenge as an opportunity and seized the moment. They would talk about how blacks were being treated throughout the nation in the North and South and how integration was a problem up North as well. However, the North wanted to focus all the attention on the South. Confusion existed throughout the nation on issues of justice and equality for all. It was a breakdown in morality.

Movements in Civility

The men of my father's generation recognized that the system was broke long before there was a Civil Rights Movement. Many had doubts about the Civil Rights Movement because in their lifetime, they were aware that the 13th, 14th and 15th amendments were not enforced, so why would they add more laws that would not be enforced. They recognized that after many veterans returned from World War II and the "Korean Conflict" circumstances had not changed. The blindfold of racism remained in control, and no one would - or could - address the matter. The source of light - the church - as stated earlier, remained adrift with her head in the sand because she was controlled by religious views. Those that would stand up and be counted were few, and their voices did not carry much weight. Darkness continued to expand. Isaiah 5:20-21-23, "Woe to those who call evil good and good evil, who put darkness for light and light for darkness, who put bitter for sweet and sweet for bitter! Who justify *and* acquit the guilty for a bribe, but take away the rights of the innocent *and* righteous from them!" (AMP).

Basic rights and laws promulgated by the founders created a level of darkness, injustice and inequality that was experienced by the men of my father's generation as it relates to their basic rights under the laws promulgated by the founders. Because of the stories told to them by their parents, stories of the action of the carpetbaggers, they were reluctant to trust northern liberals. Therefore, they placed all their trust in the Lord Jesus Christ. Psalm 118: 8-9 says, "It is better to trust and take refuge in the Lord than to put confidence in man. It is better to trust and take refuge in the Lord than to put confidence in princes."

This commitment to trust the Lord gave them the strength, confidence, faith, and grace to face every challenge without giving up, giving in, or giving out. This knowledge produced a level of responsibility and accountability that was not demonstrated by the nation or the church as a whole. This level of responsibility came down from the throne of the Father through His Son Jesus. It also gave the ability to recognize that the focus must be on the Word because it does not change. They had experienced the reality of the world's system whereby accountability was in words only. The accountability from above is sure and steadfast, as it say in Isaiah 55:11, "So shall My word be that goes forth out of My mouth: it shall not return to Me void [without producing any effect, useless], but it shall accomplish that which I please and purpose, and it shall prosper in the thing for which I sent it," and Hebrews 6:17, "Accordingly God also, in His desire to show more convincingly and beyond doubt to those who were to inherit the promise the unchangeableness of His purpose and plan, intervened mediated) with an oath." Again, the measuring stick of his love was demonstrated in his willingness to teach my father and others how to read and write.

The Father's accountability is above reproach. It is anchored, settled, and steadfast. His Word does not return to Him with a knock on the door, saying, "Mission is not accomplished." Thus, the men of my father's generation were moved to trust in Him instead of the laws of the land. The track record of this nation was like darkness to light comparable to His. This caused great confusion. The nation claims her allegiance to Him, while her action took an opposing view.

It appeared that the greatest emphasis of this nation was greed and taking advantage of the poor and those that could not defend themselves. The men of my father's generation were in this class. An essential segment of the church, not to be confrontational, backed this by proclaiming that the status quo was God ordained. The truth was obviously to anyone who read the Bible; however, truth took a back seat, or removed from the table. As said in Acts 17:26: "And He made from one [common origin, one source, one blood] all nations of men to settle on the face of the earth, having definitely determined [their] allotted periods of time and the fixed boundaries of their habitation (their settlements, lands, and abodes)," (AMP). This statement settles the issues as they relate to equality of all. We are one blood made by all ethnic groups. One blood redeemed all ethnic groups that believe in the Lord Jesus Christ.

While the founders sought to remove the concept of the caste system in the new nation, they actually expanded it as it related to slavery. In doing this, they removed the value of the blood of Jesus Christ. We know that the founders of this nation, as well as the founders of the caste system in Europe, and the slaves from Africa were all slaves to sin. They all needed a Savior. Unfortunately, this misconception that the Europeans and the founders of this nation were more civilized than the citizens of Africa received creditability from a segment of the church; therefore - in their opinion - the status quo had the blessing of the Father. This superior thinking goes against the Word. If God made all ethnic groups out of one blood, then all ethnic groups must have the same DNA, the same Source of life.

The education of my father's generation looked beyond the status quo, and produced a focus on the Lord that was so steadfast, they refused to compromise. The salvation package consisted of: knowing His Love, Truth, Grace and faith (Romans 5:8, John 1:14 and Romans 12:3).

Chapter Three

Salvation in My Father's Generation

When Adam missed the mark, he became vile, polluted, and contaminated. The Father God is Holy. Thus, the polluted product cannot reconnect to a Holy God without God establishing the guidelines and the perimeter. The product under the leadership of religion cannot establish the means because the sin issue has not been addressed. When the Bible says, "Let us make man," each member of the Team that made the product had a role to play in the reconnecting process. The Father initiated salvation; Jesus accomplished it, and the Holy Spirit drew the believer. The demand placed on Jesus required Him to give His life, paying the full price. It says in 2 Corinthians 5:21 that, "For our sake He made Christ [virtually] to be sin Who knew no sin, so that in *and* through Him we might become [endured with, viewed as being in, and example of] the righteousness of God [what we ought to be, approved and acceptable and in right relationship with Him, by His goodness]," (AMP).

Recognizing their position in Jesus Christ gave the men of my father's generation the strength to move forward during these challenging times. These men realize that Jesus had taken their place so that they could rise and live above every challenge. As a result of this revelation, like Jesus, their lives were to be sacrificial too. A greater calling removed all the roots of fear, anxiety, and frustration. It changed their perspective about themselves as well as their families. This level of revelation captured responsibility and accountability. Serving the Lord with all their heart was the first step in taking responsibility and accountability. Serving one another with the love of the Lord was a responsibility that moved them on every level- a level whereby their relationship with the Lord Jesus took priority over everything, including the hostile environment that treated them like second-class citizens. This relationship with the Lord Jesus provided them a peace that passed all understanding: peace to smile when everyone else was frowning, a peace that produced joy when there was an opportunity to be sad. It produced a peace that enabled them to love their enemies when the natural emotion was to hate. This level of peace was described by the Prophet Isaiah in Isaiah 26:3: "You will guard him and keep him in perfect and constant peace whose mind [both its inclination and its character] is stayed on You, because he commits himself to You, leans on You, and hopes confidently in You" (AMP). In this verse, the Father will guard the person and keep him or her in constant peace when the focus is on Him. This means that no circumstance or situation can pull one out of peace if the peace of the Father is within him. This level of peace, which is a product of grace, gave these men the ability to turn the other cheek and show the will of the Father through their actions.

Prayer was a major factor in their lives. There was prayer every Sunday morning at the Macedonia Baptist Church and there were individual prayers at home. My sister and I would listen intently as my father would pray every night, acknowledging that Jesus Christ was King of kings, and Lord of lords. Prayer at church on Sunday morning would focus on one particular scripture, 2 Chronicles. 7:14: "If My people, who are called by My name, shall humble themselves, pray, seek, crave, and require of necessity My face and turn from their wicked ways, then will I hear from heaven, forgive their sin, and heal their land," (AMP).

Humility Brings His Grace

The power of prayer is so important, but an element of prayer is overlooked, and that is being humble. Humbleness gives access to grace, and grace releases undeserved and unmerited favor. "My people" in the scriptures denotes the church, a church that prays and seeks after Him and not just the things from Him- a church that places great emphasis on pleasing Him and knowing Him. A church that places Him above everything else, including the government of a democracy, or the government of the people. Only then will the sin of the nation be forgiven and the land healed. This explains why the nation is in the condition she is in now as well as then. When I look back at the history of the country, I wonder why this scripture was not the focus scripture prior to the Civil War and the Civil Rights movement. It seems that the church placed greater value in the government of democracy than the government of the Lord Jesus Christ. The church now, as well as then, has aligned herself with political parties, placing her trust in either the Democrats, or the Republicans. Both parties it seems are driven by greed, self-interest and power. It is no wonder that the men of my father's generation, along with others, suffered from a lack of prayer on behalf of the church.

Pride

Pride has been demonstrated throughout this nation's history, and a segment of the church has been in the middle of it. Notice, when pride exists, the Father takes a stand against it. If the Father sets Himself against a people their unity will not be sufficient. Their unity sustains the pride, and the condition grows worse. Pride is the enemy to prayer. Pride means that faith is not a factor, or that I deserve what I am asking for. Pride is a characteristic of Satan himself. Isaiah 14:13-14 says, "And you said in your heart, I will ascend to heaven: I will exalt my throne above the stars of God; I will sit upon the mount of assembly in the uttermost north. I will ascend above the heights of the clouds; I will make myself like the Most High," (AMP). Great emphasis is placed on self. The above scriptures reveal that the nation was operating from a spirit of pride, and this spirit of pride shaped the total environment. Pride stems from the fact that one ethnic group sought to present itself as superior, while declaring that others were inferior. This very notion worked to the enemy's advantage because this attitude reflected his thinking. Pride in any form is a trait of the power of darkness, and pride tends to expand itself. A heart rooted and grounded in pride is in opposition to the teaching of the Lord Jesus. Psalms 101:5 says, "Whoever slander his neighbor in secret, him will I put to silence; whoever has haughty eyes and a proud heart, I will not tolerate," (NIV).

The courageous men of my father's generation nullify the pride of others by walking in the highest level of love. While others were magnifying themselves and the works of their hands, these men were magnifying the King of kings and His finished work. Their humility was like a magnet. Grace was the end result, and grace gave them an ability that others didn't have. The focus of pride is on one's self, and the works of one's own hands. Therefore, all the honor and glory go to self. Humility, on the other hand, focuses on the fact that all the honor and glory go to the One that purchased our redemption. A prideful heart is saying that the product has reached parity with God; therefore, the product has the right to take pride in his or her accomplishment. Pride in one's ethnic means of showing excessive self-value while devaluing others. Pride is also saying that a particular ethnic group was given something that others don't have. It is saying that God gave this ethnic group an advantage over another ethnic group. This concept contradicts the scripture, Romans 2:11, "For God shows no partiality [undue favor or unfairness; with Him one Man is not different from another]," (AMP).

Faith

A courageous stand of integrity, accountability, faith, and good

Men of My Father's Generation

work ethics were the makeup of the standard of the men of my father's generation. Integrity to their faith in the Lord Jesus Christ and refusing to allow the hostile environment to control them was consistent with what he Bibles states: "The just shall live by faith" (Hebrews 10:38). Therefore, faith in Lord Jesus Christ was priority for them. There was faith to remain faithful to their belief despite the great opposition, faith to look beyond the natural, faith to see into the realm of the spirit, and faith to recognize that the status quo did not identify them. There was faith to allow the finished work of the Lord Jesus Christ to become their reality, and it was from there that they began to say what He said about them. They had faith to trust in Him. Proverbs 3: 5-7 says, "Lean on, trust in, and be confident in the Lord with all your heart and mind and do not rely on your own insight or understanding. In all your ways know, recognize, and acknowledge Him and He will direct and make straight and plain your paths. Be not wise in your own eyes; reverently fear and worship the Lord and turn [entirely] away from evil," (AMP). This is a solid motto to live by and to instruct others.

Trusting in the Lord removed the desire to hate, to be bitter or to be angry. As they trusted in the Lord, they developed confidence in Him and in His Word. As a result of confidence in Him, their emotions were under control, and they refused to allow their emotions to damage their faith. The level of confidence went beyond their heads and took root in their hearts. Their actions were ordered of the Lord, and as a result, He ordered their steps. They disciplined their hearts and minds so that all the emphasis was placed on Him. This enabled them to recognize opportunities where others only saw obstacles. Again, we must remember that His ways are higher than man's ways, and His thoughts are wiser than the thoughts of man. Because He was the source of their trust, they had a huge advantage. This attitude reflects the heart of people that think in their heart that they have reached a level of parity with God. They seek all the honor and glory and think, "Look what we have done." The Declaration of Independence, the Bill of Rights and the Constitution are the works of man's hand. All the hands that participated in this matter were not clean hands; the hearts didn't reflect the heart of the Lord Jesus; therefore, a valuable trait was missing. The valuable trait was having a relationship with Him, the Head of the Church, the One who came into the world with grace and truth and established the end from the beginning. Isaiah 46: 9-10 says, "[Earnestly] remember the former things, [which I did] of old; for I am God, and there is no one else; I am God, and there is none like me. Declaring the end and the result from the beginning, and from ancient times the things that are not yet done, saying, My counsel shall stand, and I will do all My pleasure and purpose," (AMP).

The challenge that the product faces as it relates to his decisions and plans is that he does not have access to what he needs. The product doesn't have access to the heart of those charged with the responsibilities of executing the laws. The prophet Jeremiah reveals a powerful truth about the heart of the product. Jeremiah 17:9-10 says, "The heart is deceitful above all things, and it is exceedingly perverse and corrupt and severely, mortally sick! Who can know it [perceive, understand, be acquainted with his own heart and mind? I the Lord search the mind, I try the heart, even to give to every man according to his ways, according to the fruit of his doings," (AMP). These verses tell us that the best intention of the heart is deceitful. The heart is perverse and corrupt. The heart of a man does not have the ability to perform justice, equality and righteousness. The seed of darkness is always producing the fruit of darkness, and a tree is known by its fruit. A corrupt tree cannot produce faultless fruit. The notion that man could execute justice and equality on his own is reprehensible.

The men of my father's generation knew that it was impossible for the system - without Divine intervention - to fulfill what it had advocated. The product - man - is a spirit that resides in a body, and the product has a soul. The laws promulgated by the product have good intention, but the product does not have the ability to carry them out. The church, on the other hand, has been given the assignment of producing light, but light cannot be released when the drink is spiked by darkness. The darkness that contaminated light gives off the notion that the True Light has given His approval to the status quo. Sadly, a segment of the church has taken a page from politicians in her election to take a faulty stand. True Light takes a stand based on truth and not what is politically incorrect. An aspect of the church now, as well as then, seeks to address darkness through political action instead of operating in the power given to the church. 1st Corinthians 2:4-5 says, "Behold! I have given you authority and power to trample upon serpents, and scorpions, and [physical and mental strength and ability over all the power that the enemy [possesses]; and nothing shall in any way harm you. Luke 10:19 says, "And my language and my message were not set forth in persuasive (enticing and plausible) words of wisdom, but they were in demonstration of the [Holy] Spirit and power [a proof by the Spirit and power of God, operating on me and stirring in the minds of my hearers the most holy emotions and thus persuading them]. So that your faith might not rest in the wisdom of men (human philosophy), but in the power of God," (AMP). It is these words that energized the men of my father's generation to place their faith and their confidence in the power of His Word. They could recognize the power that He had given them, which was the power to rise above the circumstances, power to walk in authority, and power to take dominance in a subtle way. They recognized that the gospel of Jesus Christ was the gospel that was demonstrated with power, meaning that they were given power. One of the assignments given to Adam was to subdue and walk in dominion.

James Thornton

In the environment in which I grew up, one never heard of the landlord taking advantage of someone's wife or daughter. However, in my father's generation, such actions were done consistently with impunity. Yet the men of my father's generation understood their authority as believers and, therefore, they remained strong in the Lord and in the power of His might in the midst of the torture they and their families often suffered. They understood that Jesus Christ was the means by which this was accomplished. When He is removed out of the loop, the church has no power; therefore, the action of the product is of no value. Thus, when religion has control of the church, the church is not able to execute dominion. Light becomes darkness, darkness becomes light, and a lack of spiritual discernment results in truth being compromised. This was evident when the church willingly supported, sustained, and embraced the status quo because of her blindness. From a natural perspective, humanity wants to do what is right in its sight, but without the power of Truth it cannot be done. Truth requires intimacy, and without intimacy, truth cannot release freedom. Therefore, when one group is held hostage, or when one group is denied its freedom, then all groups are held in bondage. Abraham Lincoln commented on this during his Campaign Speech in 1858 to the Republican delegates during the Republican State Convention in Springfield, Illinois: *"A house divided against itself cannot stand. I believe this government cannot endure permanently half-slave and half-free. I do not expect the Union to be dissolved – I do not expect the house to fall - but I do expect it will cease to be divided. It will become all one thing or all the other."*[1] President Lincoln paraphrased the following passage from the Bible, Matthew 12:25, when he spoke of a house divided: *"And Jesus knew their thoughts, and said unto them, Every kingdom divided against itself is brought to desolation; and every city or house divided against itself shall not stand."* Thus, it is not the will of the Father for a nation to exist half slave and half free. The bondage that was inflicted on the sons and daughters of

---

1   Lincoln, Abraham. "House Divided Speech." 1858.

former slaves left its mark on those executing the bondage. The mark was not seen by the natural eye because of tunnel vision. The leader's hearts were hard and corrupt; as a result, they were "having eyes but seeing not and having ears but hearing not."

The Courage to Move Forward

The courageous men of my father's generation had to discipline themselves so that the current condition did not leave a lasting effect. Their challenges consisted of either rejecting or supporting the laws of the nation that were supported by the local church, or they placed their confidence solely on the Bible. They had to choose to trust a God that cannot be seen with the natural eyes or to trust the church that claimed she represented Him. They thankfully chose to trust the Lord and put their total trust in Him. Psalm 118:8-9 and Joshua 24:15d, say, "It is better to trust and take refuge in the Lord than to put confidence in man. It is better to trust and take refuge in the Lord than to put confidence in princes," (AMP). Joshua 24:15d continues, "But as for me and my house, we will serve the Lord." These men established the spiritual climate and commitment in their home. They remained steadfast to their conviction and mindful that there were individuals in the church who sought the gifts and not the Giver of the gifts.

Courageous men of my father's generation remained focused, looking to Jesus, the Author and Finisher of their faith. It was through this commitment and dedication that they were prevented from being bitter and filled with animosity. Grace, the unmerited favor of Jesus Christ, played a vital role in their everyday life. In the midst of all the confusion, the abuse of power, the lies and the corruption, Grace changed the focus. They maintained that no system of this world - even with support of a segment of the church - would hold them down. Their marching orders were to allow the Words of the Lord Jesus to identify them. They were in the world, but not of the world. Though their flesh wanted to react, the Grace that was in them, as a result of the finished work of the Lord Jesus placed a demand on them to take responsibility. This level of responsibility consisted of keeping their minds focused, guarding their hearts, and giving Grace the opportunity to do the work.

This level of responsibility was based on the knowledge that the heavenly Father loved them; the Father initiated their salvation, Jesus accomplished their freedom, and the Holy Spirit was their teacher. The Father's love as revealed in 1 John 4:10-11 is this: "In this is love: not that we loved God, but that He loved us and sent His Son to be the propitiation (atoning sacrifice)for our sins. Beloved, if God loved us so [very much], we also ought to love one another," (AMP). In the midst of this hostile environment, many could still comprehend that He loved them and had a purpose for their lives. Jesus accomplished it all, Romans 8:2, 10 says, "For the law of the Spirit of life [which is] in Christ Jesus [the law of our new being] has freed me from the law of sin and of death. But if Christ lives in you, [then although] your [natural] body is dead by reason of sin and guilt, the spirit is alive because of [the] righteousness [that He imputes to you]," (AMP). Jesus is the Giver of life, and the life giving that comes from Him is superior to the law of sin and death. He took their sins, our sins, the sins of the oppressors and the sins of the whole world to the cross with Him.

The total freedom that comes from Him is predicated on believing in Him, and that He finished the work. Being sensitive to the Holy Spirit gave Him access to teach them. He testified of the finished work of the Son. You see, the men of my father's generation refused to be removed from their conviction despite their living condition, or despite an aspect of the church siding with the status quo. Their foundation was rock solid; their strength was renewed every day. Opportunity availed itself to them to give up,

Men of My Father's Generation

give out or to give in, but they remained strong in the Lord and in the power of His might. This steadfastness was manifested in all aspects of their lives; a mentality whereby the principles of Jesus Christ took priority over their feelings, over hurts, over being disrespected, and over being de-valued. Serving others became the order of the day even when they were rejected while serving. I had two uncles who served in the Army, and their service was above reproach. They served their country well and then returned home and submitted to the local authority. The level of sin was so obvious that a blind person could recognize it, yet the government of this nation continued to ignore the injustice and the iniquities. Truth remained adrift, hiding under the cover of tradition and religion. Courage required them to forget, forgive and move forward (Philippians 3: 13-14). For them, their salvation was from Jesus, the One who purchased them.

Chapter Four

Grace in My Father's Generation

Grace has to be received. It is not earned. The grace in these special men empowered them to work and walk through great challenges. Grace was made available to all, but few chose to give grace the opportunity to work and maximize its assignment in them. The whole nation needed the gift of grace because of the division within the nation. The church needed this grace because it would place the church in a position whereby she could provide the light to the world and salt to the earth. The concept, "one nation under God" could not be achieved without the presence of grace. The Bible is very clear in John 1:17: "For while the Law was given through Moses, grace [unearned, undeserved favor and spiritual blessing] and truth came through Jesus Christ," (AMP). This favor established a level playing field. No one group was superior to another, and no one group was inferior to another. Grace removed the ability to judge others because all have sinned and fallen short. Grace gives the receiver of grace the ability to walk in total forgiveness, and this is what this nation needed. The southern states had hatred toward the northern states; the sons of slaves had bitterness and anger toward those that were held in bondage. This was a mountain that could not be removed by government or democracy, and because of a lack of knowledge, the church - the source of light - could not produce what was needed. The nation was at a standstill, but a grace opportunity was available to all, and this grace was provided by the Father through His Son. It says in Matthews 11:27-28, "All things have been entrusted and delivered to Me by My Father, and no one fully knows and accurately understands the Son except the Father, and no one fully knows and accurately understands the Father except the Son and anyone to whom the Son deliberately wills to make Him known.

Come to Me, all you who labor and are heavy laden and overburdened, and I will cause you to rest. [I will ease and relieve and refresh your souls]," (AMP).

Civil War

Notice, the invitation was directed to those that were heavy laden and overburdened. The group was seen by their own nation as inferior. The other group saw itself as superior. But families from both groups lost loved ones in the last generation because of one of the greatest tragedies known to this nation, and humanity as a whole- the Civil War. The war was the result of brothers fighting against one another because of a lack of knowledge and a failure of leadership by the church. Everyone was broken in some form or fashion. Isaiah 5:13 says, "Therefore, My people go into captivity [to their enemies] without knowing it and because they have no knowledge [of God]. And their honorable men [their glory] are famished, and their common people are parched with thirst," (AMP). The "honorable men" represented the church leadership, and the church leadership was without knowledge. The men of my father's generation recognized this major flaw, and so they were forced to look for a system of government that was above reproach, and that system of government was the government of Jesus Christ. In this system of government, the King has already provided what is needed. Every provision has been established in Him, and His way is superior to the ways of man. The prophet Isaiah received profound revelation in Isaiah 55:7-9, where he says, "Let the wicked forsake his way and the unrighteous man his thoughts; and let Him return to the Lord, and He will have love, pity, and mercy for him, and to our God, for He will multiply to him His abundant pardon. For My thoughts are not your thoughts, neither are your ways My ways, says the Lord. For as the heavens are higher than the earth, so are My ways higher than your ways and My thoughts than your thoughts," (AMP). It is obvious that the thoughts of the church, and the leaders of the nation were in total opposition to His thoughts.

Again, the courageous men of my father's generation were the receivers of grace, even if they were not aware of His (Jesus) name. They knew they had favor, and that favor was from the Lord. They knew intuitively that something gave them the ability to walk in love, forgiveness, peace, patience, and self-control. These were not natural traits; they were divine. These traits displayed the characteristics of the Lord Jesus Christ, and favor was released as a result of these traits. Favor was the opportunity to love the Lord and to love their enemies, despite the fact that the enemy displayed no love for them. We must remember that the product is saved by grace. Ephesians 2:8 says, "For it is by free grace [God's unmerited favor] that you are saved [delivered from judgment and made partakers of Christ's salvation through [your] faith. And this [salvation] is not of yourselves [of your own doing, it came not through your own striving], but it is the gift of God," (AMP). This grace empowered them to look beyond the status quo, beyond the government and beyond what they were taught in the local church. This grace gave them the ability to focus on Jesus Christ: Jesus Christ, the Savior, the Lord, and the Author and Finisher of their faith. This grace gave them the ability to renew their minds. This grace gave the ability not to allow the circumstances to identify them. This grace gave them the ability to be mindful that they were heirs of God, and joint heirs with Jesus. Knowledge of this position placed them in a position whereby they knew that He was their Source, and that His grace gave them access to opportunities that they did not have before. As a result, they chose to take advantage of the opportunities and accept the fact that achieving was a matter of receiving what He has accomplished for them. They saw opportunities where others saw only obstacles and could release love where others released hate. Giving grace the opportunity to work and maximize its assignment in their lives propelled them to reach levels that even the more educated individuals could not reach. In essence, it was not them, but the grace that was working in them. Therefore, grace is the enabler.

Moses and Paul had one thing in common. They allowed grace to maximize its assignment in their lives. In Exodus 33:17, it says, "And the Lord said unto Moses, I will do this thing also that thou has spoken: for thou has found grace in my sight, and I know thee by name," (KJV). 1 Corinthians15:10 says, "But by the grace [the unmerited favor and blessing] of God I am what I am, and His grace toward me was not [found to be] for nothing [fruitless and without effect]. In fact, I worked harder than all of them [the apostles], though it was not really I, but the grace [the unmerited favor and blessing] of God which was with me," (AMP). As a result of the grace that worked in them, Moses' request was answered. He said, "Show me your glory," and, as a result, he was given access to knowledge that others did not have. He wrote the first five books of the Old Testament. Paul was given access to sights and sounds that others didn't have. He wrote two-thirds of the New Testament. While none of the men of my father's generation had the revelation of Moses or Paul, they did have access to a power that enabled them to rise above their challenges and impacted those in their generation and generations to come. It was the Father's grace that empowered them. It was the Father's grace that enabled them to maintain a position of responding instead of a position of reacting. They displayed His glory by looking beyond the natural and accepting the responsibility of being mentors to all that would learn from them, blacks as well as whites.

I remember someone saying to my dad, "How can you love these folks?" His reply to them was, "I love them- meaning white folks - because the Lord first loved me." It is that attitude that best represents the courageous men of his generation. This is the attitude whereby they wanted to make sure that their children had a better life than them. The better life was one in which their children chose to receive the Lord Jesus and maximized their assignment in life. This consisted of recognizing why the Lord sent them to earth, releasing the potential that He placed in them, fulfilling His purpose for their lives, and reaching the destiny that He ordained for them. They recognized that releasing the potential, fulfilling His purpose, and reaching the destiny that He ordained was, in essence, releasing His glory. They recognized releasing their potential didn't necessarily mean material gain, but knowing Him and the power of His might. They also recognized that His glory can only be released when He is giving the higher level of praise and appreciation. In my father's time, God's glory was prevented from being fully manifested because the product (men) were more concerned with expressing their glory and the works of their own hands. The Prophet Isaiah received profound revelation on this matter in Isaiah 42:8: "I am the Lord; and that is My name! And My glory I will not give to another, nor My praise to graven images," (AMP). The shocking thing to remember is that if it does not represent Him, it does not display His glory. If His glory is not displayed, this means that He is not involved. It may look like Him and have the support of the masses and be highly esteemed, but as it says in Luke 16:15, "But He said to them, you are the ones who declare yourselves just and upright before men, but God knows your hearts: For what is exalted and highly thought of among men is detestable and abhorrent [an abomination] in the sight of God," (AMP).

My parents told us a story after story of how the Lord provided and protected their relatives. This was an action of grace. In fact, the environment that my father grew up in was controlled by the grace of the Lord Jesus Christ. The family that raised him was a product of the grace of the Lord. My father was the recipient of so much grace from the Lord Jesus that his life actually mirrored that of a white person from that era. It has been said that wherever he worked, he would always be in charge. The favor that he received from the Jernigan family was a direct result of the grace the Lord Jesus gave him everywhere he went. While there were many horrible stories told as to what was going on throughout the nation, my family never suffered any of them. It was not the goodness of my father, nor the goodness of the Jernigan's family, but the grace of the Lord Jesus displayed on all of them. Romans 5:20 says, "But where sin increased and abounded, grace [God's unmerited favor] has surpassed it and increased the more and superabounded," (AMP). In the midst of this ungodly environment, grace was given a change and worked in all that gave it a chance. The Holy Spirit has made me aware of the hand of grace in the lives of my father and men of his generation as a result of the teaching on grace by my Pastor, Dr. Hart Ramsey. His teaching on grace has changed the whole perspective and proves that grace gives all of us the ability to walk in love.

When normality is in opposition to truth, truth has to be sought out by whatever means are necessary. Proverbs 23:23 says, "Buy the truth and sell it not; not only that, but also get discernment and judgment, instruction and understanding," (AMP). This means truth must be protected. An extreme high value must be placed on truth. The total package of truth could be released without grace. Truth without grace would place the product in a position where there was no hope. John 1:14 says, "And the Word [Christ] became flesh [human, incarnate] and tabernacled [fixed His tent of flesh, lived awhile] among us; and we [actually] saw His glory [His honor, His majesty], such glory as an only-begotten son receives from His Father, full of grace [favor, loving-kindness and truth," (AMP). The favor of grace and the availability of truth gave the product what was needed for success. This process was essential in the lives of those men, for truth says all have sinned. All have missed the mark. Truth says God loves us first, and we must love Him. Truth says we must love one another, and if normality opposes truth, we must stand for truth. Truth says we must not only stand for truth, but we must also be able to recognize truth. Truth says it wants to change the reality, but truth knows that this can be accomplished without grace.

These courageous men knew from within that if they were to impact their generation and others to come, then truth and grace must be received so that the two could work together. Grace and truth gave them the ability to overcome the odds, recognize opportunities, and seize moments. They were able to seize the moment by focusing on the Promisor and His promises. Their motto was Philippians 4:13: "I have strength for All things in Christ, Who empowers me [I am ready for anything and equal to anything Through Him Who infuses inner strength unto me; I am self-sufficient in Christ's sufficiency," (AMP). They had the grace to receive the Truth.

Chapter Five
God's Strength Through Prayer in My Father's Generation

A significant challenge for the men of my father's generation was the leaders maintaining the zeal for religion, and placing such a high value on democracy that truth and righteousness were placed low on the priority list. This attitude of the nation reveals the attitude that was expressed many years ago. Romans 10:3 says, "For being ignorant of the righteousness that God ascribes [which makes one acceptance to Him in word, thought, and deed] and seeking to establish a righteousness [a means of salvation] of their own, they did not obey or submit themselves to God's righteousness," (AMP). The fingerprint of this attitude can be traced throughout history. The product dismissed the ways of the Father while embracing his own ways. This attitude says the product has reached the same level of God; therefore, his opinions, ideas, and concepts are just as valuable as God's. The men of my father's generation had to remind themselves daily that they were in the world, but not of the world. They had to take a righteous stand in the midst of a great opposition.

The righteous stand consisted of taking on responsibilities beyond their scope of influence and standing in the gap for others, including those in authority. My father's duties involved increasing, stabilizing and mentoring others. By reminding them that the system was not above reproach and that the teaching of the Lord Jesus took priority over the system of this world, they had to fulfill a responsibility few Christians expressed: praying for those in authorities – both those you supported and those that you did not support. 1st Timothy 2:1-3, says, "First of all, then, I admonish and urge that petitions, prayers, intercessions, and thanksgiving be offered on behalf of all men. For kings and all who are in positions of authority or high responsibility, that [outwardly] we may pass a quiet and undisturbed life [and inwardly] a peaceable one in all godliness and reverence and seriousness in every way. For such [praying] is good and right, and [it is] pleasing and acceptable to God our Savior," (AMP). This Christian trait has for so long been missing. The tendency is to pray only for those that one supports. I have with my own ears heard ministers of the gospel make statements like, "I can only pray that he is removed from his position." This was the position that many ministers of the gospel took during Eisenhower's' presidency- praying for wicked police chiefs that everyone knew abused people of color while denouncing President Eisenhower for sending troops to Little Rock to enforce the law. There were people praying for leaders that didn't enforce the law, but not praying for leaders that enforced the law. Now, remember the benefits for praying for those in authority, "A peaceable one in all godliness and reverence and seriousness in every way." Could it be that a lack of peace is the result of not praying? The men of my father's generation had complete peace even though they were living in a hostile environment. They not only had peace, but they had confidence that status quo would change. This change would not be the result of the system waking up one day, and saying that it was wrong, but change would be the result of divine intervention.

Prayer

Men of my father's generation remembered the power of praying. Prayer was as natural to them as breathing. Prayer was a source of strength. Prayer gave my father the ability to look beyond the natural and to focus on things above. Prayer prevented him and others from giving in to the pressure they were bound to endure. Luke 18:1 and 1 Peter 4:7-9 say, "Also [Jesus] told them a parable to the effect that they ought always to pray and not to turn coward [faint, lose heart, and give up. But the end and culmination of all things has now come near; keep sound minded and self-restrained and alert therefore for [the practice of] prayer. Above all things have intense and unfailing love for one another, for love covers a multitude of sins [forgives and disregards the offenses of others]. Practice hospitality to one another [those of the household of faith]. Be hospitable, be a lover of strangers, with brotherly affection for the unknown guests, the foreigners, the poor, and all others who come your way who are of Christ's body.] and [in each instance] do it ungrudgingly [cordially and graciously, without complaining but as representing Him]," (AMP). The men of my father's generation had to be rooted and grounded in truth in order for survival. The above scriptures revealed the heart of Jesus Christ as it relates to prayer and relationship.

The emphasis was on love and the role that love plays in dealing with sin, for love enables us to forgive. The combination of prayer and love in my father's relationship was a model that everyone should seek. The importance of showing love to strangers speaks volumes as it relates to our hearts. I remember as a child that my father would bring hitchhikers to the house and provide them with food and money. Prayer empowered them to work all day and set up most of the night with a sick person in the community. Prayer and love enabled them to use their resources to help the poor and others in need.

How the Ability to Give Transformed a Community

One of the many skills of my father was farming. He would send an invitation to all and any to come to the farm and gather as many vegetables as they needed. He would actually gather the vegetables for the old and sick, black or white. He had an incredible giving spirit. My mother said, "He would give away more than we made." He lived by the motto set forth in Acts 20:35: "In everything I have pointed out to you [by example] that, by working diligently in this manner, we ought to assist the weak, being mindful of the words of the Lord Jesus, how He, Himself said. It is more blessed [makes one happier and more to be envied] to give than to receive," (AMP). Giving was in my father's DNA. To him, helping others was as important as living. He constantly reminded us that Jesus gave all that we might live and live in victory. My father was a natural giver, but his knowledge of truth and righteousness elevated his giving. His giving was a product of his praying. His giving was an expression of his love. His giving was a process by which his giving was a seed that produced a harvest for his children. Giving left his hands, but it always returned with a huge harvest. His giving became contagious and impacted the whole community.

Many of the men of the community would give their free time to help others. The giving of godly wisdom to those in the community was as consistent as the giving away of goods and resources. This spirit of giving went beyond the county line; wherever there was a need, many men of my father's generation sought to provide what was needed. These men were less talk and more action. In addition to offering physical help, the men of my father's generation sought to bring Jesus Christ back into His church. The tendency was to focus on religion, tradition, denomination and the government under the leadership of democracy. In the minds and thinking pattern of many, the teaching of the Lord Jesus would be implemented through the government. If it was not implemented within the authority of the government of democracy, it could not be achieved. The problem with that concept is that not everyone in government had the heart of the Lord Jesus. Remember, democracy rules from the bottom up. It cannot be achieved through religion because not every religion acknowledges Jesus Christ. It cannot be achieved through denominations because each denomination has its own perspective. The only means by which the gov-

Men of My Father's Generation

ernment of Jesus Christ is activated is through Him. He is the Head of the church. It is His church.

The church is not owned by religion. It is not owned by tradition, nor is it owned by denomination. Neither is it owned by the government of democracy. It is not owned by the Christian Right, the Christian Left, the conservatives, or the liberals. It is not owned by the Apostles, the Prophets, the Evangelists, the Pastors, or the Teachers. These are gifts that He gave to the church. These gifts were given for a specific reason after He ascended upon high as revealed in Ephesians 4:8,12-13: "Therefore it is said, when He ascended on high, He led captivity captive [He led a train of vanquished foes] and He bestowed gifts on men. His intention was the perfecting and the full equipping of the saints [His consecrated people], [that they should do] the work of ministering toward building up Christ' body [the church]. That it might develop until we all attain oneness in the faith and in the comprehension of the full and accurate knowledge of the Son of God, that [we might arrive at really mature manhood [the completeness of personality which is nothing less than the standard height of Christ's own perfection], the measure of the stature of the fullness of the Christ and the completeness found in Him," (AMP).

It was God's strength that gave the men in my father's generation to stand. It was His strength that enabled them to pray, even when it appeared the prayer did not manifest in the natural- they still prayed for their fellowman, their community and their enemies. It was God's strength that enabled them to love and give out of their lack and abundance. Psalm 29:11 puts it so eloquently, "The Lord will give [unyielding and impenetrable] strength to His people; the Lord will bless His people with peace," (AMP).

Chapter Six
Identity Crisis of the Church and Man in My Father's Generation

Throughout their lives, the men of my father's generation were faced with a negative view of themselves. This view of was equated to a seed planted in the earth that produced great harvests. The harvest of hopelessness, anger, frustration and lack of knowledge concealed their true identity. The combination of a negative view of themselves and lack of identity left most in a state of total confusion. It also had a devastating consequence: They began questioning the credibility of the church, God, and the validity of His Word. This gave access to religions such as Islam (the black Muslims), which taught that all whites were evil and that Jesus Christ was not the Son of God. The door was open to this demonic spirit because of a lie that was told at the outset. The lie was blacks are subhuman, or inferior. It is no wonder that during the time of my father, Elijah Mohammed and the black Muslims grew exceedingly fast by spreading their doctrine. The enemy knew that many young blacks were prime targets for this kind of radical teaching. First of all, the Christian church refused to teach the Gospel of Jesus Christ when blacks and people of color were discussed or declared. The picture of our Savior was depicted by the church as blonde, blue-eyed and white. Even though this does not reflect His true natural identity, this picture of Him has been impressed in the minds and hearts of the people since this nation was created. Islam represented to the blacks a more accurate picture.

Because of the characteristics, attitudes, and position of the whites in this nation, and displaying Jesus Christ as the same, a significant number of blacks and other ethnicities rejected Him. My father and the men of his generation recognized that neither the government nor the church represented Him. They had to discipline themselves not to be deceived by a particular religion or the government. They had to reject the teaching of the Muslims, even though this specific religion depicted a picture whereby people of color were seen in the Koran. They had to reject the possibility of unity for the first time within the blacks. They understood that this wasn't the unity bringing God and His Body together as one. This unity was the result of the church not being accountable to what thus said the Word.

The fact remained that injustice, and a lack of equality existed in the North and South. The blacks in the southern states were denied the opportunity in many cases to exercise their ability to vote, and the blacks in the northern states had no need to vote because the condition would remain the same. One cannot comprehend the frustration that they faced- frustration because of hopelessness. It was professed by the nation as a "melting pot" that promised freedom, and equality for all, and yet, a vital percentage of the population never experienced the promises.

No matter how much the nation or the churches profess freedom and equality for all; it was obvious that this level of unity and accountability didn't exist for all. (Neither does it today.) It is equally true that the church now, as well as then, is not fully functioning according to her purpose, or according to His plan. It was true then and it is true now, that certain groups within the church seek to perpetuate their own opinions, concepts and ideas while the standards of the Head of the church are being ignored in the name of freedom of religion. The government of the Lord Jesus Christ is superior to every government of this world, including the government of democracy. *And* it is in this area that the men of my father's generation had their greatest challenge.

We say that we are a Christian nation, but the principles of democracy take a higher place in the agenda than the teaching of the Lord Jesus. Freedom of speech under democracy takes a higher position than the principles of the Lord Jesus, whereby He declares that our communication should minister grace to the hearer. Ephesians 4:25 says, "Therefore, rejecting all falsity and being done now with it, let everyone express the truth with his neighbor, for we are all parts of one body and members one of another. Let no foul or polluting language, nor evil word nor unwholesome or worthless talk [ever] come out of your mouth, but only such [speech] as is good and beneficial to the spiritual progress of others, as is fitting to the need and the occasion, that it may be a blessing and give grace [God's favor] to those who hear it," (AMP).

The directive given, in Ephesians 4:29 is not obeyed in the church among brothers and sisters in Christ, and the attitude of the church has impacted the attitude of the nation. A segment of the church has placed greater value on freedom of speech as outlined in the Constitution than the Word as revealed by Jesus, the Head of the church. In this setting, men of my father's generation had to discipline themselves to focus on the truth of the Word more than on the doctrine of man. We must remember that each denomination and religion shares one thing in common: each has its own take of what the Bible says. Each is strongly influenced by tradition, and each places great value on the thoughts of the product while placing less value on the words of God. This means that if they agree with the Bible, then it had high priority; if they don't agree, it has little or no priority. The Bible is clear that out of one blood, He made all ethnic groups and out of one blood, all ethnic groups that believe were redeemed by and with the same blood.

In the hearts of the men of my father's generation, this question had to be addressed. If one blood made all ethnic groups, and one blood redeemed all ethnic groups, then why does one group think it is superior to all others? Was the blood that redeemed the other ethnic groups contaminated? If the blood that redeemed the other ethnic groups was contaminated, then salvation for other ethnic groups would have to be contested by the power of darkness. All ethnic groups had to be redeemed because none was righteous. All started out the same way, and the only means by which all could be saved was by the blood of Jesus. The word salvation in the Greek is the word "soteria," which means deliverance or being delivered from something to something, Romans 1:16 says, "For I am not ashamed of the Gospel [good news] of Christ, for it is God's power working unto salvation [for deliverance from eternal death] to everyone who believes with a personal trust and confident surrender and firm reliance, to the Jew first and also to the Greek," (AMP). The "Gentiles" are all ethnic groups that were not Jews.

My father was persuaded by the Word that he and those that stood with him were part of God's original plan. They were not an afterthought. Jeremiah 29:11 says, "For I know the thoughts and plans that I have for you, says the Lord, thoughts and plans for welfare and peace and not for evil, to give you hope in your final outcome," (AMP). This means that the heavenly Father has thoughts about each person, and He has a plan and purpose for each. This means that no one is insignificant. Each person is valuable to Him. By understanding this, it required them to place discipline on what they heard, and what they were taught. In this process, they had to be able to reject the status quo while receiving without question the unchangeable Word written in the Bible. This requirement required more than natural skills. It could only be achieved through the Holy Spirit. John 16:13 says, "But when He, the Spirit of Truth [the Truth-giving Spirit] comes, He will guide you into all the Truth [the whole, full Truth]. For He will not speak His own message [on His own authority]: but He will tell whatever He hears [from the Father; He will give the message that has been given to Him], and He will announce and declare to you the things that are to come [that will happen in the future,"

Men of My Father's Generation

(AMP).

The Holy Spirit is not a thing. The Holy Spirit is the Third person of the Trinity. He was there before the product was created. The Father said, "Let us make man." The "us" consisted of the Father, the Son, and the Holy Spirit. There has been an erroneous understanding of the Holy Spirit; thus, the value that He brings to the table has been overlooked. The Holy Spirit empowered the believer, and the Holy Spirit provides Truth that neither seen nor recognized in the natural state of the product.

Truth's Power

The men of my father's generation sought the truth, and they recognized that the level of truth that they were seeking could not come from man. And as valuable as education was, this level of truth could not be revealed through education. This level of truth could only be accessed through and by the Source of Truth - the Father - who is the God of Truth. Truth is one of His greatest attributes. His Truth is superior to all forms of government in this world's system. Zeal for His Truth placed a demand on my father's generation; the current situation, the words of others, or the attitude of a segment of the church could not circumvent their desire for the truth. Now, the enemy's objective was to use the environment and the status quo to his advantage by negatively impacting the next generation. Remember the environment was pregnant with hatred, bitterness, anger, greed, and an unforgiving spirit. It was a great climate for the power of darkness. Even though these emotions were justified, based upon treatment they endured, the Spirit of Truth reminded them that each negative seed of anger would produce a harvest. This is so because every seed produces after its kind, and as long as the earth remains, there will be a seedtime and a harvest for that seed. We see what the seed of bitterness produced in the Civil War and the longevity of that seed's harvest. Today, the harvest of the seed of hatred is still producing fruit. The harvest of the seed of greed impacted the nation then, and today, we are still reaping the harvest. They were also mindful that as a nation, there was no repentance for these sins. In Romans 6:23a, it says, "For the wages which sin pays is death," (AMP). If sin is not repented, the sin remains, and it produces death." The men of my father's generation were reminded that confessing their sins produced forgiveness. 1 John 1:9 says, "If we [freely] admit that we have sinned and confess our sins, He is faithful and just [true to His own nature and promises] and will forgive our sins [dismiss our lawlessness] and [continuously] cleanse us from all unrighteousness [everything not in conformity to His will in purpose, thought, and action," (AMP).

The challenge that this nation has had from the outset is that she does not recognize her sins, and as a result, she doesn't confess her sins. While the old saints didn't have the spiritual knowledge that enlightened leaders have today, they knew the value of confessing their sins. (In a church where predominately blacks attend, confessing sin was and *still* is a standard of the Christian lifestyle.) Confessing is an acknowledgment that one or a nation has missed the mark, and that the nation or the individuals need forgiveness. In other words, the product is asking God, the Father, for forgiveness for his or her lawlessness, or the lawlessness of a nation. Confessing is also an acknowledgment that God is superior to the product, and that the product was born in sin. Failing to do so is a violation. 1 John 1:10 says, "If we say [claim] we have not sinned, we contradict His Word and make Him out to be false and a liar, and His Word is not in us [the divine message of the Gospel is not in our hearts]," (AMP).

The men of my father's generation would read the Word and talk about what they read daily. They would ask questions and make statements concerning the credibility of the church. We must remember the church consists of all that believe in Jesus Christ and all that have accepted Him as Lord and Savior, regardless of race or gender. The difficulty for the church now, as well as then, is that when Jesus is removed out of the circle, a substitute comes in dressed as Him and subjugates the body. This substitute uses the ideas, concepts, and opinions of the body, and the body is pleased with its contribution. The principles that Jesus preached have been disregarded and seen as another opinion. The enemy used what was available to him - freedom of religion.

Religion embraced God, but denied the value of the Son. Religion sells the notion that the product can reconnect to God through his own knowledge and means. The fact remains in this nation that what the product saw as a valuable tool became a liability. Luke 16:15 says, "But He said to them, you are the ones who declare yourselves just and upright before men, but God knows your hearts. For what is exalted and highly thought of among men is detestable and abhorrent [an abomination] in the sight of God" [Amplified]. Freedom of religion was seen by the masses as a courageous trait that must be maintained. The challenge with that position is that Jesus Christ didn't come to earth to establish a religion. He came to restore a relationship. His relationship cannot be established through or by religion. It is instead a relationship whereby He is the only way to the Father. There may be many ways to Him, but only one way to the Father. The challenge for religion is that it does not address the sin issue, so religion cannot remove the consequences of Adam's sin.

The church is empowered by the grace of Jesus Christ and the Holy Spirit. When allegiance is given to religion, the power to subdue and walk in dominion has been removed. Under these conditions, the church is on her own. Isaiah 42:8 says, "I Am the Lord; that is My name! and My glory I will not give to another, nor My praise to graven images," (AMP). Thus, the original assignment given to the church to be light to the world and salt to the earth cannot be accomplished. His glory is the essence of Who He is. The men of my father's generation understood that the church was given power, and if that power was executed, then the status quo would have to change. Because the church had concluded that this system of government was ordained of the Lord as a result of being controlled by religion, the consensus was that the changes would have occurred within the boundaries of the government. We must remember that the Father will not give His glory to another. If power was released, then religion would be the one receiving the glory. Religion is a product of the flesh. 1 Corinthians 1:29 says, "That no flesh should glory in His presence." Yet, throughout the history of this nation, the tendency has been to place such great emphasis on the founders as if they were above reproach. Even when the decisions were made that were totally opposite of His word, a segment of the church remained silent and indifferent towards the truth. When truth is absent, darkness rules with impunity. The men of my father's generation saw the real deal. They recognized that there was a lack of credibility in the church. The church declared the teaching of the Lord in their mouth, but the demonstration of her action was just the opposite.

This lack of power impacted the believer in every aspect of life, the sons of former slaves, as well as the sons of former slave owners. The product created in the image and likeness of the Trinity could not function according to the plans and the purposes of the Manufacturer. The power to love, to respect, and treat others as they wished to be treated was out of their reach. This concept emphasized that one ethnic group was superior to all other ethnic groups and that the other ethnic groups were created to serve the superior group. Another concept that has connection to the caste system of Europe stresses that blacks do not have the intellectual ability to provide for themselves.

The negative ideas, opinions, and concepts were never challenged by the church because the church was suffering from a deficit of power. The Gospel of Jesus Christ includes the power of Jesus Christ. Matthew 28:18 and 1 Corinthians 2:4 says, "Jesus approached and breaking the silence, said to them, all authority [all power of rule] in heaven and on earth has been given to me. And my language and my message were not set forth in persuasive [enticing and plausible] words of wisdom, but they were in demonstration of the [Holy] Spirit and power [a proof by the Spirit and power of God, operating on me and stirring in the minds of my hearers the holy emotions and thus persuading them," (AMP). The essence of the above scriptures is that the product cannot function according to the plan and purpose of God without the presence of the Holy Spirit, coupled with the grace of the Lord Jesus. The product must comply with the manual if the product is to function properly. When the power of the Holy Spirit is removed, the product is working in his or her own strength, and this is not sufficient. The power of the Holy Spirit coupled with Grace gives one the ability to live in the finished work of the Lord Jesus: loving one another, respecting one another and thinking of the other person more highly than self are all evident when the trait of pride is removed.

The great tragedy for this nation, then, is seeking to accomplish its mission while rejecting the power of the Holy Spirit, and the grace of the Lord Jesus. It was impossible to live in peace, to walk in love, honor, and unity and respect others, and to execute justice working within the limitations of a flawed and powerless product. The great deception is that this nation had accomplished a great achievement in removing Hitler from Europe, and the victory went to their heads. This achievement was a source of pride; however, at home, injustice and second-class citizenship ruled with impunity. It didn't move the liberals, the conservatives, the Democrats or the Republicans, and obviously, it didn't move an aspect of the church.

Jesus Christ makes a powerful declaration in Matthews 16:15-19: "He said to them. "But who do you say that I am? Simon Peter answered, "You are the Christ, the Son of the living God." And Jesus said to him, "Blessed are you, Simon Barjona, because flesh and blood did not reveal this to you, but My Father who is in heaven. I also say to you that you are Peter, and upon this rock [revelation] I will build My church; and the gates of Hades [hell] will not overpower it. I will give you the keys of the kingdom of heaven; and whatever you bind on earth shall Have been bound in heaven, and whatever you loose on earth shall have been loosed in heaven," (NAS).

The church has been given power that is superior to the power of any government including the United States. The church refused to execute this power while magnifying the power of the nation. The gates of hell shall not prevail against the church when the church executes the power given to her by the Lord Jesus. The church has been given the keys to the kingdom with the ability to bind and loose: bind racism, loose justice and equality, exposed the lies, and proclaim the truth. It is in this setting that the men of my father's generation lived their lives; again, the source of light refused to produce light to the world, and unwillingness to preserve the principles of the Lord Jesus. Hidden in their refusal was the notion that the status quo on earth was the status quo in heaven, and, therefore, there was no need to bind and loose. Now, one would have to be blind in both eyes to reach this conclusion, and this explains why, to this day, hatred and bitterness remain. A lot of the venom released is toward the church because it lost its identity. It had an identity crisis. This identity crises affected both the church, the men of my father's generation, and mankind as a whole. This was a great challenge in my father's generation. Today, it's still a great challenge

Chapter Seven
Finding True Identity Brings Humility in My Father's Generation

While this book is about the men of my father's generation, my mother made me aware of the favor that she received as a result of the Lord's grace during this period of time. Being the product of a single parent and working at nine years old as the head of the family, she too received favor from God from many white families. My father's life, as well as my mother's story, portrays that there were whites who didn't live by the status quo, but lived by godly Christian principles. Not all of the stories of how the southern states have been depicted by many northern theories are true. They were many whites standing in the gap. Compassion was displayed in many ways by many white folks. In the local environment that my father grew up in, it was the norm because of how he was treated. Outside of the local environment, he and others saw the wounds of racism, but he refused to allow those negative traits to identify him. 1 Corinthians 15:10 says, "But by the grace [the unmerited favor and blessing] of God I am what I am," (AMP). When my mother and father allowed grace to work in them, grace revealed their true identity. Their true identity is what God has said about them. The true identity of the product can never be identified by another product. The true identity can only be identified by the Manufacturer (God) of the product. This one truth was an agent in dismantling all the erroneous thoughts that kept many in bondage, even to this very day. The Emancipation Act removed the legal bondage, but could not remove the spiritual bondage. Only through His grace can the product enjoy the benefits of true freedom.

While a great emphasis was placed on the removal of the legal bondage, it could not set the captive free. On the other hand, believing that you were superior to all other ethnic groups didn't make you free either. While there was no legal impediment, the majority was still controlled by a spiritual force that they were not even aware of. This force placed them in the same boat as the slaves, or the ex-slaves- in bondage. Thus, total freedom is the removing of sin. John 8:31-24 says, "So Jesus said to those Jews who had believed in Him, if you abide in My word [hold fast to My teachings and live in accordance with them], you are truly My disciples. And you will know the Truth, and the Truth will set you free. They answered Him, we are Abraham's offspring [descendants] and have never been in bondage to anybody. What do You mean by saying, you will be set free? Jesus answered them, I assure you, most solemnly I tell you, whoever commits and practice sin is the slave of sin," (AMP).

Herein lies the great deception of sin: thinking that you are free because of obeying the law, when in fact, the laws of Moses do not make one right with the Lord Jesus. Having the benefits of total legal freedom didn't make one free from the bondage of sin. This truth levels the playing field because all have sinned and missed the mark. This deception is hard at work today among the conservatives and the evangelicals that speak as if they are the only ones who have the corner on truth. The same individuals remained silent when injustice was ruling with impunity, and racism was expanding its territory. Thus, the lack of truth has propelled this country into the greatest division since the Civil War. This division is the result of the church not producing light. This division is the result of a segment of the church in bed with both political parties. This division is also the result of political ideology becoming the god of many on both sides of the political spectrum. The Christian Right and the Evangelicals teamed together and elected individuals who shared their conviction, thinking that the product in him or herself had the solution to a spiritual illness. The team removed the power of prayer and repentance. James 4:10 says, "Humble yourselves [feeling very insignificant in the presence of the Lord, and He will exalt you [He will lift you up and make your lives significant," (AMP).

The men of my father's generation refused to give the power of darkness the last word. They refused to allow racism, hatred, bitterness, second-class citizenship, poverty and the power of religion to have the last word. They believed that the power of love would always prevail over the above negative traits. Proverbs 10:12 and 1 Peter 4:8 say, "Hatred stirs up contentions, but love covers all transgressions. Above all things have intense and unfailing love for one another, for love covers a multitude of sins [forgives and disregards the offenses of others," (AMP). The sin natural to humanity is such that loving someone or something that has harmed, hindered, and shown disrespect is beyond the ability of the product. Doing so cannot be achieved through religion. In the governments of the world, it is outside of the range of the product. But as discussed earlier, this is not a learned love. This level of love requires the product to be born again, born from above. This process requires the product to give the Son total control. The Son is the only means by which the product can be born from above. The spiritual birth is superior to the natural birth. Therefore, the spiritual birth gives the product the ability to walk in love. In reality, when Jesus has been given total access to the heart and soul, it is He that demonstrates this level of love. The love these men demonstrated was not them, but the love of the Father in them. The love of the Father is expressed in the Son. Ephesians 3:19 says, "[That you may really come] to know [practically, through experience for yourselves] the love of Christ, which far surpasses mere knowledge [without experience]; that you may be filled [through all your being] unto all the fullness of God [may have the richest measure of the divine Presence, and become a body wholly filled and flooded with God Himself," (AMP). You see, His divine presence enabled them to express His kind of love without wavering when they were rejected and even cursed.

When the opportunity availed itself for them to be bitter, angry and frustrated, grace stepped in and said, "I got your back." When persecution reached its highest level, and they were thinking about throwing in the towel, the Holy Spirit reminded them that they persecuted Jesus Christ. He was persecuted, and He suffered for humanity in that He gave His life, and everyone who lives for Him will suffer. It says in 2 Timothy 2:12 and 1 Peter 2:21 that "If we suffer, we shall also reign with Him; if we deny Him, He also will deny us. (1 Peter 2:21) "For Christ also suffered for you, leaving you [His personal] example, so that you should follow in His footsteps," (AMP). The suffering and persecution they received came from within, from family members and from others. These men were mindful that disciplining what they heard and saw would be critical to their survival. They had to monitor their hearts and minds daily. They had to address thoughts and wounds below the threshold of their conscience. The seed of love had to cultivate every day in them. Everything that impeded its growth had to be removed. Every weed and rock that opened the door to offense had to be removed. Peace was their goal. It was essential to their survival. Psalm 119:165 says, "Great peace have they who love Your law; nothing shall offend them or make them stumble," (AMP). They made a decision to guard what they heard and never let negative words identify them, even when the "n" word was used. The love of the Lord Jesus was so rooted and grounded in them that negative words of others prompted them to pray and to extend more love. Love is a product of His grace, and humility opens the door to more grace. Maintaining a humble spirit gave them access to more love, patience, and compassion. They took advantage of every opportunity to walk in love and to pray for those that abused them and those that spoke evil against them.

Men of My Father's Generation

It is my honest belief that the prayers of these courageous men kept their environment free from some of the extreme acts of hatred demonstrated in other parts of the state. It was said by someone that Mr. Jernigan made it known to the KKK that they were not welcome in the community. I never heard my father or the other men of his generation tell stories of the acts of the KKK in the community. From this observation, one can conclude that whites, as well as blacks, stood against the activities of the KKK. This was the result of seeking to please the Lord. Men of my father's generation - both blacks, as well as some whites - had to place a guard at the door to their heart and soul, refusing to allow the status quo to influence them. Truth and knowledge of His undeserved grace had to be rooted in their heart. Faith, mercy, and peace also had to take a seat in the heart, but also in every department of the soul. The soul consists of the following departments: the mind, the will, the emotion, the imagination, and the intellect. The mind had to be renewed. Romans 12:1-2 says, "I appeal to you therefore, brethren, and beg you in view of [all] the mercies of God, to make a decisive dedication of your bodies [presenting all your members and faculties as a living sacrifice, holy [devoted, consecrated] and well pleasing to God, which is your reasonable [rational, intelligent] service and spiritual worship. Do not be conformed to this world [this age,] fashioned after and adapted to its external, superficial customs], but be transformed [changed] by the [entire] renewal of your mind [by its new ideals and its new attitude], so that you may prove [for yourselves] what is the good and acceptable and perfect will of God, even the thing which is good and acceptance and perfect [in His sight for you]," (AMP). This process required them to give His truth priority over the status quo, including religion, tradition and all that they were taught.

Knowledge of His unconditional love and being mindful that society and the laws of the product cannot measure His love placed a demand on them to focus their attention on Him. In Him they lived, and looked to Him. 1 Peter 3:22 says, "[And He] has now entered into heaven and is at the right hand of God, with [all] angels and authorities and power made subject to Him," (AMP). He was the Source of their strength, wisdom, knowledge and understanding. This level of love was made known to all that placed their trust in Him. His love motivated those whites in the community and sons of slave owners to change their perspective, for out of one love, He made all ethnic groups. In the Jernigan family, this truth was planted in each family member, and as a result, wherever a family member was, they demonstrated this love. This kind of love forced them to separate themselves from their extended family that didn't have the same conviction. Placing my father in positions of authority was an expression of the Agape love. This love was contagious; it left its fingerprint on all that would receive it.

Unfortunately, many were so rooted and grounded in hatred, and the bitterness and anger that saturated the environment that this kind of love displayed by the Jernigans and other families produced more hatred. We must remember that this kind of love could not be released without the head department of the soul, the mind being renewed. If the mind is not renewed in truth, then hatred, bitterness, and anger intensified to such a degree that it impacted all the departments of the soul. This explains why such evil could exist and rule with impunity. The minds of those executing the laws were not renewed. This speaks volumes about all these men who were willing to disregard the status quo and the teaching of religion in order to believe and accept the teaching of the Lord Jesus. Human nature seeks to take the path of least resistance. They took the path of extreme resistance and stood their ground.

They chose to believe. Choosing to believe unlocks the door to great blessings, but it also unlocks the door to great consequences. Believing means erroneous information must be removed. Removing erroneous information means the minds have to be renewed. Renewing the minds means positive information has to replace negative information, as the negative information shapes how a person or persons sees themselves and others. Renewing means that the new information is superior to the old. The new information is from God. The old information is from the product. The origin of this old information is not from the product. It is from the power of darkness. The product was the student. The new information is from God, and the product (man) is still the student; but, the new information is superior in all aspects to the old. The new information grows the child into a man. It says in 1 Corinthians 13:11: "When I was a child, I talked like a child, I thought like a child, I reasoned like a child; now that I have become a man, I am done with childish ways and have put them aside," (AMP). A child seeks to display his or her own will. A child is immature and selfish, and because of the sin nature from Adam, a child has a natural tendency to disobey. Paul's analogy is saying that manhood is not determined by your age, but by having a true relationship with the Father. However, because of a lack of knowledge, many assume that manhood was based on age and not on truth. The fact remains that a man can be in his fifties in age, but has a child-like mentality. True manhood is recognizing that there is a greater source of knowledge and truth, and being willing to submit to His authority.

The men of my father's generation walked in of knowledge and understanding. They put away everything that did not please the Father, everything that took an opposing view of the teaching of the Lord Jesus Christ. They put away the religious spirit that distorted the truth and renounced the lie that said one ethnic group was superior to all others. They put away the notion that one ethnic group had the corner on truth. They put away the ideas, concepts, and opinions that played such a valuable role in establishing the caste system in Europe. They put away the spirit of greed and exploiting the poor. They put away the notion that government of democracy is superior to the government of the Lord Jesus Christ. They put away the notion that the government of this nation has the ability to address the needs of the total person. They put away the unwillingness to be committed to honor one's own words. They put away the erroneous doctrine that the opinions of the people take priority over the words of God. They put away youth ideas that sought to compromise the truth. They grew into men of truth and righteousness, men of spiritual understanding. They grew into men of wisdom. Proverbs 2:10-12 says, "For skillful and godly wisdom shall enter into your heart, and knowledge shall be pleasant to you. Discretion shall watch over you, understanding shall keep you. To deliver you from the way of evil and the evil men, from men who speak perverse things and are liars," (AMP). Manhood opens the door to wisdom, knowledge and understanding.

True manhood is able to recognize and appreciate the wisdom, knowledge and understanding of the Father. True manhood has an eye for the truth and is able to identify truth over a lie, identify light over darkness, and identify life over death. True manhood enables the real man to lead and to be extremely sensitive to the Holy Spirit. True manhood knows that the ways of the natural man are in opposition to the ways of God. Proverbs 14:12 says, "There is a way which seems right to a man and appears straight before him, but at the end of it is the way of death," (AMP).

Obligation

A child is not able to recognize the ways of darkness and death. A child is not able to identify a lie. A child sees no difference in darkness and light, death and life. Under the guides of a youth, deception has free access. The motto expressed by the men of my father's generation was, "Boy, grow up and become a man." This motto was taught to those of my generation as we were growing into manhood and taking responsibility. The great tragedy of the Emancipation Act was that no one taught them the responsibilities of being a man. No one taught them that freedom demands responsibilities. No one gave them a true and full picture of the totality of freedom. Bondage was their way of life for so long that it became the only reality they knew. The reality of freedom and responsibility was as foreign to them as learning a new language. The nation failed in two areas: lack of preparation and failing to execute the laws that they passed. The ex-slaves and their descendants were in a no-win position. Failure was inevitable without divine intervention. However, because of His grace, truth, and mercy, divine intervention was released when the men of my father's generation sought Him. Matthew. 6:33 says, "But seek [aim at and strive after] first of His entire kingdom and His righteousness [His way of doing and being right], and then all these things taken together will be given you besides," (AMP).

The challenge for the product has always been to seek for things and not the Giver of the things. As we said earlier, this is what happened with the founders. They sought to establish a government free of the stings of the caste system, but did not seek God. The focus was on establishing a government controlled by the people instead of focusing on Jesus and His kingdom, which would have been all that was needed.

Placing God second meant that there was another desire that was preferred over Him, which is a violation of His word. It says in Exodus 20: 3-4 "You shall have no other gods before or besides Me. You shall not make yourself any graven image [to worship it] or any likeness of anything that is in the heavens above, or that is in the earth beneath, or that is in the water under the earth," (AMP). When the product creates something and places it before Him, it becomes an idol. 1 Chronicles 16:16 says, "For all the gods of the people are [lifeless] idols, but the Lord made the heavens," (AMP). Anything that the product makes and is placed above Him becomes a stumbling block.

With the track record of this country, religion and the church, the men of my father's generation had to focus their attention on Him if they were to rise above the circumstances and challenges that were before them. Because of the presence of the Holy Spirit, they knew that the status quo could not work and that the product was insufficient in wisdom, knowledge, understanding, and spiritual insight. In other words, they had a zeal and a desire for the truth that could only come from the Source of all truth, the heavenly Father. They had a diligent devotion for Him to such a degree that winning was the only option. As a result, the guiding force in their lives was the Bible, and they refused to compromise. Again, the commitment was so intense that they chose the Lord Jesus over family members, over religion, and over an aspect of the church. Whites were standing up for blacks, and blacks were standing up for other blacks when it could cost them their lives. They were sold on the truth that for them to live was Christ, to die was gain (Philippians 1:21), and to be absent from the body was to be present with Him (2 Corinthians 5:8). Serving others and proclaiming His principles took priority over everything. Taking responsibility was the mark of a higher calling.

Taking responsibility and seizing the moment placed these men above others and their ideas. Taking responsibility required them to change their focus from things of this world to things above. Taking responsibility required being led by the Holy Spirit, placing all their trust in the Lord. Being led by the Holy Spirit shifted the focus from them to a higher power, meaning they were in the world, but not of the world. Focusing on the Lord Jesus allowed them to become doers of the word and not hearers only. This meant that the living word produced in them a desire to please the

Father and to live in the reality of the finished work of the Lord Jesus. Living in the reality of the Lord Jesus Christ required the heart, as well as the soul, to be filled with all the fullness of Him. The evidence that this had taken place was in the ability to look beyond the natural, the ability to focus on things above, the ability love their enemies, and the ability to pray for those that took advantage of them. It was evident in the ability to choose the way of light and life over darkness and death. Another aspect of the new life in Christ Jesus was thinking and reasoning. Philippians 4:8 says, "Finally, brethren, whatsoever things are true, whatsoever things are honest, whatsoever things are just, whatsoever things are pure, whatsoever things are lovely, whatsoever things are of good report, if there be any virtue, and if there be any praise, think on these things," (KJV). There was a paradigm shift to the positive things and the things written in His word. The circumstances didn't control their thinking, and neither did the negative voices of others. They maintained positive thinking when the opportunity was available to think negatively. The power of positive thinking took priority over all the negative thinking. They refused to allow the negative to identify them. In other words, they lived above the situations and circumstances.

Their reasoning was rooted and grounded in hope and faith and sustained by His grace. As a result, the gift of hope and faith combined with His grace placed them in a position to see beyond the natural. Hope means a desire of something good with the expectation of obtaining it. While faith is being persuaded and confident in the truth of the Father's word and in His ability to perform according to His promise, Hebrews 11:1 says, "Now Faith is the assurance [the confirmation, the title deed] of the things [we] hope for, being the proof of things [we] do not see and the conviction of their reality [faith perceiving as real fact what is not revealed to the senses," (AMP). 1 Peter 3:15 says, "But in your hearts set apart Christ as Lord. Always be prepared to give an answer to everyone who asks you to the reason for the hope that you have. But do this with gentleness and respect," (NIV). The men of my father's generation became aware that in giving a reason for their positive attitude, they had to have respect. Even their enemies recognized the fact that they showed respect when in the natural; respect should not have been the first choice.

Respect was always forthcoming because they had a thankful heart. They were thankful that their names were written in the Lamb's Book of Life. They were thankful for their personal relationship with the Lord Jesus, a relationship that elevated them to sons, 1 John 3:1 says, " See what [an incredible] quality of love the Father has given [shown, bestowed on] us, that we should [be permitted to] be named and called and counted the children of God! And so we are! The reason that the world does not know [recognize, acknowledge] us is that it does not know [recognize, acknowledge] Him," (AMP).

The father-son relationship was highly significant because many had no knowledge of their natural father. The Father-son relationship was based on kinship; thus, the relationship reached a high level in that the sons could communicate with the Father as His sons. The joy of knowing the heavenly Father, and having a personal relationship with Him, provoked the men of my father's generation to maintain their position. Their position, then, was secured by the blood of Jesus Christ, the Author and Finisher of their faith. The position in Him empowered them; it gave them patience, identity and strengthened their faith, which allowed them to see beyond the natural. This generation of men of all ethnicity was vital to the survival of this nation. It was not so much the residual aspect; it was the value that they placed on the Word, and the finished work of the Lord Jesus Christ. This position impacted their work ethic in taking responsibility and shaping their view of life. Their stand provided light in an environment that was

Men of My Father's Generation

dominated by darkness. Their joy produced strength. Nehemiah. 8:10 says, "Nehemiah said, "Go and enjoy choice food and sweet drinks, and send some to those who have nothing prepared. This day is sacred to our Lord. Do not grieve, for the joy of the Lord is your strength," (NIV). The evidence that this statement is truth is that throughout the life of my father, I never heard him complain. Nor did I hear any of the other men complain. They were mindful of the credibility of His Word, the Father's unyielding love, and His faithfulness.

It says in Lamentations 3:22-23, "It is because of the Lord's mercy and loving-kindness that we are not consumed, because His [tender] compassions fail not. They are new every morning; great and abundant is your stability and faithfulness," (AMP). It is amazing what a person can endure when one is empowered by the Father's Grace and by the Holy Spirit. The supernatural becomes the norm, and the impossible becomes possible, and the finished work of the Lord Jesus Christ becomes their reality. The outside challenge never rises above the capability or the capacity of the empowerment that is rooted in the heart. Thus, the challenge really provokes what is already established in the heart.

Each challenge presented to them had a choice, either to give in, give up, or give out, but they chose to stand on truth. The legs of truth were stronger than every challenge. The legs of truth always sustained them. The legs of truth came with the power of grace. Thus, every challenge was at a huge disadvantage. The combination of Grace and Truth provided them with the victory that went beyond their natural understanding. While truth revealed the heart of the Father, grace provided His favor. Opportunities were given without explanation, and favor and mercy were present when recompense was due. My father acknowledged that favor and mercy ruled over justice and walked hand in hand on their behalf. The favor that they received from the Father was the product of His grace. James 4:6 says, "But He gives us more and more grace [power of the Holy Spirit, to meet this evil tendency and all others fully]. That is why He says, God set Himself against the proud and haughty, but gives grace [continually] to the lowly [those who are humble enough to receive it.]," (AMP).

His great grace impacted their mindset, attitude, and demeanor so that they remained humble even when they were abused and misused. Humility brought to the table a trait that was very difficult to explain or comprehend; therefore, the recipients of humility were greatly confused and left the table scratching their heads. Humility placed a demand on them to think, to question themselves and their positions. Notice the lateral part of the above verse, "God sets Himself against the proud and haughty." This meant that the proud and haughty must deal with the Manufacturer for demonstrating these traits. In other words, there is a consequence for their action, and they are aware of the consequences. The New American Standard Bible says, "God is opposed to the proud." Deep down in the heart of every recipient of grace, is the knowledge that God was not pleased. Pleasing the Father was the objective of the men of my father's generation. Remaining humble was their way of life.

Chapter Eight

Acknowledging the Father in My Father's Generation

Again, seeking to please the Heavenly Father was the desire of the men of my father's generation, both black and white. Sons of former slaves, as well as sons of former slave owners had this one commonality: pleasing Him. This required them to do a daily evaluation of their lives. This required them to acknowledge that they had missed the mark and that Jesus was the only means by which salvation was available. This acknowledgement forced them to evaluate the value of religion and what they had been taught. It forced to them to recognize and accept the fact that many things they were taught were lies. These lies were the product of teachers having a zeal for God, but the zeal was compromised because of a lack of knowledge. These teachers sought to elevate their religion over the principles of the Lord Jesus Christ. These teachers sought to bring to the table their own righteousness while disconnecting themselves from the righteousness established by the Father through His Son. A righteousness that gives one right standing with the Father is as the scripture says in Matthew 6:33: "But seek [aim at and strive after] first of all His kingdom and His righteousness [His way of doing and being right], and then all these things taken together will be given you besides," (AMP). This particular verse spoke volumes to the men of my father's generation. His righteousness takes priority over everything, so His righteousness must be the focus. This means that religion and tradition fall short of meeting the requirement.

Aiming for Him would be the only means by which they would have total success, total freedom, and total peace. This truth impacted them in their everyday activities. Proverbs 3:6-7 says, "In all your ways know, recognize, and acknowledge Him, and He will direct and make straight and plain your paths. Be not wise in your own eyes; reverently fear and worship the Lord and turn [entirely] away from evil," (AMP). God empowered them to obey this commandment. This requirement forced them to come out of the comfort zone to place Him above the status quo, above tradition and religion. His principles took priority over what was accepted by the masses. It was in this setting that they were able to recognize that evil was controlling the environment and that this evil was the product of darkness. They recognized that when Jesus Christ is in control, light and life control the individuals as well as the environment. They recognized that truth, justice and equality cannot be achieved by the product. Truth can come from only one source. The freedom package consists of total freedom. Galatians 5:1 says, "In [this] freedom Christ has made us free [and completely liberated us]; stand fast then, and do not be hampered and held ensnared and submit again to a yoke of slavery [which you once put off]," (AMP). This scripture enlightened them to the fact all humanity was enslaved to something. While slavery placed many in legal bondage, sin placed all humanity in spiritual bondage. The laws promulgated by the product could not remove the spiritual bondage that held humanity as hostage. Paul asked a question in Romans 7:24-25: "O unhappy and pitiable and wretched man that I am! Who will release and deliver me from [the shackles of] this body of death? O thank God! [He will!] through Jesus Christ [the Anointing One] our Lord! So then indeed I, of myself with the mind and heart, serve the Law of God, but with the flesh the law of sin," (AMP).

Familial Duty

The common enemy that has set his sight on all humanity, sought to expand its territory through selfish means. Men who thought that being popular with the opposite sex would share themselves

Men of My Father's Generation

with every woman available. However, men of my father's generation reminded them that the true definition of manhood was responsibility. Fatherhood is an arena of responsibility that began before the child is born. Having children outside the marriage didn't remove the responsibility. They reminded them that many of them came up without a natural father, suffering the consequences of that action. They encouraged them to reframe from being a sperm donor, but to become a son of the heavenly Father so that they could become the husband and father that He called them to be. They also reminded them of the negative trait of responsibility that had already taken root in many of them. On the plantation, the male slave either had little or no responsibility in caring for his offspring; thus, planting seed was all that was required.

This spirit of a lack of responsibility rested in the hearts of many. Therefore, grandfathers, uncles, ministers of the Gospel and others in the community took on the role of mentorship. These courageous men saw evidence of this consequence in their community. They realized that if this trend continues, then the next generation will be in greater bondage and that this level of bondage would perpetuate itself. Many of these men who rejected responsibility would say, "I am free, I can do what I want." The response from the men of my father's generation was that freedom demands responsibilities. This position took courage, but they remained steadfast to their conviction in advocating the huge responsibilities placed in the father's hand. Proverbs 22:6 says, "Train up a child in the way he should go [and in keeping with his [or her] individual gift Or bent], and when he is old he will not depart from it," (AMP). This is the father's responsibility.

Fatherhood denotes kinship. Kinship automatically means responsibility. The heavenly Father took responsibility for the product created in His image and likeness. It was He that initiated the salvation plan. Jesus carries it out, and the Holy Spirit draws each person. The prophet Isaiah got access to the record in heaven in Isaiah 53:10: "Yet it was the will of the Lord to bruise Him; He has put Him to grief and made Him sick. When You and He make His life an offering for sin [and He has risen from dead, in time to come]. He shall see His [spiritual] offspring, He shall prolong His days, and the will and pleasure of the Lord shall prosper in His hand," (AMP). These plans were established before the product was created.

Responsibility takes place before the child is born. Since the Heavenly Father took responsibility in addressing every need for His product, should not the body do likewise? The nation is suffering today because of failing to take responsibility years ago. Taking responsibility is the result of knowledge, light, truth, and discernment. Farmers know if they are to receive a good harvest, responsibility must be taken in cultivating the ground before planting the seed. Many natural seeds like individuals are planted, but lack of cultivation hinders productivity. The founders didn't see the value of all; therefore, the potential and purpose placed in them by God was aborted. The founders, the earthly fathers and the farmer who planted the seed without cultivation have one thing in common: they are agents of abortion.

Remember, it is the fathers who must take that responsibility: fathers of the nation, earthy fathers and the farmer, Deuteronomy 30:19 says, "I call heaven and earth to witness this day against you that I have set before you life and death, the blessings and the curses; therefore choose life, that you and your descendants may live." Ephesians 6:4 says, "Fathers, do not irritate and provoke your children to anger [do not exasperate them to resentment], but rear them [tenderly] in training and disciple and the counsel and admonition of the Lord," (AMP). The blessings are predicated on choosing the way of the Lord. Making this choice requires the

Men of My Father's Generation

fathers to take responsibility. Taking responsibility means seeking the wisdom from God. The righteous choice has great benefits. It impacts generations that follow with positive information. Rejecting the righteous choices means death, and curses are the downfall of the generations that follow.

Many children today are exasperated and resentful because fathers failed to take responsibility in rearing up their children in accordance to the word. It appears that more children are abandoned today by their natural fathers than in any time in previous history of our country, to include the Civil War. This abandonment is not only depicted in black males, but white males as well. When fathers reject responsibilities, it shapes the thinking and action that being the "sperm donor" becomes the norm and government provision for the children abandoned by their natural fathers has become a way of life. The men of my father's generation observed this trend in their generation, and they knew through the Holy Spirit that if it was not removed it would yield such a negative result. They placed a demand on themselves to eradicate this enemy by making themselves available to all that would accept their mentorship. This trend was so indelible that many children called their mentor "Uncle," thinking that he was their blood uncle because of his love, patience and concern for them. Hosea 4:6 says, "My people are destroyed for lack of knowledge, I will also reject you that you shall be no priest to Me; seeing you have forgotten the law of your God, I will also forget your children," (AMP).

The generations that preceded the men of my father's generation had access to modern technology - an incredible advancement - but there was a deficit in truth because of the responsibility issue. The paradox was that the product made great accomplishments in technology, but could not overcome the power of sin. Thus, each proceeding generation had access to the accumulation of knowledge, but remained separated from truth, righteousness and relationship. This was one of the concerns of the men of my father's generation, and it was expressed in their zeal to reveal the truth. Many times when they gathered and prayed they would quote Matthew 24:12: "And the love of the great body of people will grow cold because of the multiplied lawlessness and iniquity," (AMP). The Greek word for iniquity is the word "Anomia," and it is defined as a transgression of the law, or being lawless: not having, knowing, or acknowledging the laws of the Manufacturer. Again, the church as well as the nation is facing many challenges today because of a lack of leadership in the area of responsibility that took place many years ago.

Misconception

Many of the men of my father's generation recognized the fact that the church, as well as the nation had gotten off course. This direction would lead the church, as well as the nation into greater darkness. When there is a deficit in light, darkness has total control. This is a process that is subtle and lies below the threshold of consciousness. It works its magic on all, including the majority. The majority's opinion is not free from this spirit. The thoughts of the majority become fertile ground for the power of darkness to work because the consensual in the natural is that of the opinions of the majority has an advantage. Therefore, the opinions of the majority have to be taken into consideration of the total picture, and if there was an error, someone from the majority would have recognized the error. If the heart of three or four leaders is corrupt, their corruption will contaminate the rest. Thus, the opinions of the majority have been circumvented by the power of darkness, and the heart has become desperately wicked. The heart of the majority does not have a system that protects it from a malfunction, and only God knows the content of the heart.

My father's generation recognition of the truth, wisdom and

Men of My Father's Generation

knowledge aside from reality was the working of the Holy Spirit. These were not learned men. Again, these were men one generation removed from slavery. These were men who didn't enjoy the abundant life of total freedom. These were men exploited by their own country and hated by fellow citizens. These were men whom human history has testified on their behalf as living in one of the worst environments known to humanity. These were men placed in a position to give their lives for citizens of another country while living as second-class citizens in their own country – a country that described herself as a "Christian nation" in words while using acts that could best be described as demonic in the treatment of her own citizens. They lived in a nation whose goal was to provide freedom for the whole world while refusing to execute justice and equality at home. A nation that invited the whole world to her shores, while maintaining a strategy to keep others in bondage. This plan was in the DNA of those in leadership while the church continued with business as usual without taking a righteous stand.

The plan was so evil that neither the oppressors nor the oppressed recognized the depth of the evil. The only means of surviving this level of evil was through the Holy Spirit. Jesus said in John 14:26 and Acts 1:8, "But the Comforter [Counselor, Helper, Intercessor, Advocate, Strengthener, Standby], the Holy Spirit, Whom the Father will send in My name [in My place, to represent Me and act on My behalf], He will teach you all things. And He will cause you to recall [will remind you of, bring to your remembrance] everything I have told you. But you shall receive power [ability], efficiency, and might] when the Holy Spirit has come upon you, and you shall be My witnesses in Jerusalem and all Judea and Samaria and to the ends [the very bounds of the earth," (AMP). It was the empowering of the Holy Spirit that gave them the strength, the courage, the steadfastness and the confidence to go on.

The empowering of the Holy Spirit enabled them to rise above every circumstance, every challenge. The empowering of the Holy Spirit enabled them to see opportunities where others saw only obstacles. The Holy Spirit equipped them to be strong in the Lord, and in the power of His might. This Power exceeded the power of the government, the power of fear, and the teaching of religion. The Bible states that fear is a tormenting spirit. 1 John 4:18 says, "There is no fear in love; but perfect love casteth out fear; because fear torment. He that feareth is not made perfect in love" [KJV]. The power of the Holy Spirit in revealing His Love removed the traits of fear. Thus, love takes a higher position than hate; love covers a multitude of sins. The love of the former slaves was greater than the hate of the former slave owners. The will to abide in Him exceeded the acts of government, religion and tradition, and abiding in Him gave them victory. The Holy Spirit continued to provide whatever was needed by reminding them of His faithfulness and His Word. The scriptures say, "Your faithfulness is from generation to generation; You have established the earth, and it stands fast," Psalm 119:90; "They are new every morning; great and abundant is Your stability and faithfulness," Lamentations 3:23; and "And from Jesus Christ, the faithful and trustworthy Witness, the Firstborn of the dead [first to be brought back to life] and the Prince [Ruler] of the kings of the earth. To Him Who ever loves us and has once [for all] loosed and freed us from our sins by His own blood," Revelation 1:5 (AMP). Knowing that the Father had demonstrated His faithfulness to the Son, and the Son to the Father, the men of my father's generation knew that they could depend on Him. They knew that He was dependable, and He could be trusted, therefore, their trust was in Him and not the system of man.

Knowledge of His Word and His creditability elevated them to look beyond the natural and into the realm of the spirit. Knowledge of His Word and Holy Spirit empowered them to pray for those in authority and love their enemies. It say in 1st Timothy

Men of My Father's Generation

2:1-2, "First of all, then, I urge that entreaties and prayers, petition and thanksgiving, be made on behalf of all men. For kings and all who are in authority, so that we may lead a tranquil and quiet life in all godliness and dignity," (NAS), and Matthew 5:44, "But I say unto you, love your enemies, bless them that curse you, do good to them that hate you, and pray for them which despitefully use you, and persecute you," (KJV). It was the love for the Lord and the work of the Holy Spirit that enabled them to stand in the gap for those in authority when in fact, those in authority were not standing for them. To love an enemy that was spewing out venom every time they opened their mouths was not a natural act. This was the action of the Holy Spirit. The men of my father's generation had no choice but to pray for the leadership, when in fact, many were not even able to cast their vote. This empowerment of the Holy Spirit changed their reality from murmuring and complaining to a reality of joy and peace.

It is incomprehensive to understand in the natural what they went through daily, weekly, and throughout their lives. The apartheid in South Africa is the only thing that comes close to defining the environment in which they lived. However, South Africa didn't proclaim her allegiance to the teaching of the Lord Jesus. South Africa didn't declare, "In God We Trust," or "One Nation Under God."

The mindset of these courageous men of my father's generation was to look to Jesus Christ as the example, because when they looked upon their leaders to show a Christ-like mindset, their stance was contradictory to their confession. Philippians 2:5 says, "Let this same attitude and purpose and [humble] mind be in you which was in Christ Jesus; [Let Him be your example in humility," (AMP). It was His mindset that navigated them through the turbulent seas of life so that they could intercede for the church and the nation. Through their prayers and the leading of the Holy

Spirit, many saw the Civil Rights movement before it took place. Many saw and recognized the opportunity that it would present, although many also saw it as a failure. Many saw its failure because the enemy was never flesh and blood. Many recognized the fact that the 13th, 14th, and 15th Amendments had been added to the Constitution for years ago, yet they were not enforced. Many recognized that this whole challenge was spiritual in its origin. Ephesians 6:12 says, "For we are not wrestling with flesh and blood [contending only with physical opponents], but against the despotisms, against the powers, against [the master spirits who are] the world rulers of this present darkness, against the spirit forces of wickedness in the heavenly [supernatural] sphere," (AMP).

The men of my father's generation understood by acknowledging Him, circumstances would not be ideal for them in natural per se, but they could withstand and stand their ground through the adversities, harshness, injustice and unfairness. There is a saying that the old saints would say. It goes like this, "If it wasn't for the Lord on my side, I don't know where I would be." This was the acknowledgment that they needed Him.

Chapter Nine
The Beginning of Physical Change in My Father's Generation

The generation of my father was a generation of great awakening, new technology, new inventions, knowledge, and the G.I. Bill. The cry for freedom spread throughout the nation with a familiar tone heard prior to the Civil War, but it was rejected. While an aspect of the church remained loyal to the status quo, there were political leaders on both sides who recognized that the nation was not living up to her word. They saw the inconsistencies in sending young men of color off to fight for the freedom of others while being in bondage at home. That was not a positive billboard for democracy they wanted to project. President Truman had desegregated the military, and people of color were gaining access to a better education. It appeared as if the mindset was changing and "A mind is a terrible thing to waste" became the battle cry. However, as positive these changes were, the movers and shakers were *still* focusing on the laws promulgated by the political leaders- man, and not the laws of the Heavenly Father. Once again, the nation was trying to fix a spiritual problem with a man-made solution.

These new changes gave us access to radio and television. Prior to the expansion of the Rural Electric Cooperative, Uncle PJ ran a line from his house to where we lived to ensure that we had one light in one room of the house. This one light enhanced our ability to read at night. With the expansion of the Rural Electric Cooperative, we no longer needed a kerosene lamp. As the "old folks" would say, "You are living high on the hogs." Again, these changes produced a new perspective. This was the beginning of our very own industrial revolution. This gave us access to radio, television, the movies, and new inventions. The ice box was replaced with a hot point refrigerator. Living on the Jernigan land gave us access to those new innovations. We could watch television with them, but having your own television set was something special. We were one of the first black families to have a television, and many of our extended families as, well as the church family would come over and watch the Wednesday and Friday night fights at our house.

It was during this time that my dad purchased one acre of land with the intention of building our first home. The skills that he had obtained placed him in a position to build his own home. These were exciting times, the eradication of upward mobility against the obstacles. The eradication of erroneous information that had held us in bondage was dissipating. This season of enlightenment brought to my memory the writings of Solomon in Ecclesiastes 8:1, which reads, "WHO IS like the wise man? And who knows the interpretation of a thing? A man's wisdom makes his face shine, and the hardness of his countenance is changed," (AMP). These new changes provoked a level of optimism that did not exist before. These changes also provoked a level of accountability and responsibility. The leadership trait in them wanted to seize and take advantage of the change. They were provoked to think in terms of legacy and not just for the moment. They learned to see opportunity where others saw obstacles. These changes released purpose and passion, a guiding vision that focused on the future by the people constantly praying and having a strong desire to make life better for all.

These changes gave many the opportunities to dream, and to believe for the impossible. The essence of these changes was a willingness to forgive, to live above the status quo mindful that each person was valuable, and that the common enemy was a lack of knowledge. Also, as a result of the GI Bill, the housing market soared, making jobs available to all, from laborers to skilled workers. The availability of these good-paying jobs and the new technology impacted all. From a natural perspective, this was the season of the Great Awakening. For the first time, it appeared that we were free spiritually and mentally.

The income of my father and others expanded because of the close proximity to Camp Rucker (later changed to Fort Rucker). The positive results of these changes were getting a high school education, and a college education. Both were now within our reach. The Jernigan family rented out rooms to soldiers stationed at Fort Rucker, and since we were the only black family around, the soldiers – being from all parts of the country – encouraged us as children. They made me aware of the opportunities available in the Army. This was a time of great changes, and it was also a time of great hope. The changes coupled with teaching from the Bible, making the impossible possible.

Those changes impacted the total person. The leader in each person began to manifest. The changes placed a demand to seize the opportunity, focusing on the opportunity and not the obstacles. These changes gave me access to opportunities that my dad didn't have. The opportunities consisted of going to college, or serving in the military. Going in the military gave one access to the G.I. Bill. This was a profound change that unlocked doors, giving us all lifestyles that were beyond our dreams. The changes gave us a level of truth that had been hidden. These changes provoked a desire to rise above the circumstance. These changes released a zeal that had been held in bondage- the changes revealed that zeal needed skill to be successful. These skills could be learned, and everyone benefited from the changes. A new wind of optimism spread throughout the community. The view of the south as being backward was eroding. The changes removed the indentured servant's mentality and opened the door to self-worth, and self-respect for those that saw themselves as inferior. The changes removed the spirit of dependability forcing fathers to place a demand on themselves to prepare their children for the changes. These changes sent a message to the status quo that bondage and darkness would no longer rule with impunity.

To the amazement of many, in the midst of all the changes, the church, the source of light remained as a whole silent. Psalm 127:1 says, "Except the Lord builds the house, they labor in vain who build it: except The Lord keeps the city, the watchman wakes in vain," (AMP). The ideas and concepts of the product in addressing this matter were fruitless. While the outside of the plate was clean, the inside [heart] remained corrupt. The product again found himself beating his head against a stone wall that would not fall. The modern technology and the efforts of the political leaders were no match for this spiritual sickness that had contaminated the whole nation. The contamination could not be removed by the physicians of the world because the physicians themselves were sick. This healing could only come from the Source that was greater than the sickness. Isaiah 1:4-5 says, "Ah, sinful nation, a people loaded with iniquity, off springs of evildoers, sons who deal corruptly! They have forsaken the Lord, they have despised and shown contempt and provoked the Holy One of Israel to anger, they have become utterly estranged [alienated]. Why should you be stricken and punished any more [since it brings no correction]? You will revolt more and more. The whole head is sick, and the whole heart is faint (feeble, sick, and nauseated)," (AMP). If modern technology and the unity among the political leaders didn't produce a repentant heart, the result would always be the same.

Outside of the cup is changed, but the heart remains corrupt. Repentance is the only means by which the heart can be clean. It says in 1 John 1:8-9: "If we say that we have no sin, we are deceiving ourselves and the truth is not in us. If we confess our sins, He is faithful and righteous to forgive us our sins and to cleanse us from all unrighteousness," (NAS). The challenge for the nation

Men of My Father's Generation

in refusing to acknowledge the sin means that truth was not in them for all those years and that they were deceived. Failing to acknowledge the sin says that the Civil War was a just war, when, in fact, it could have been avoided. James 5:16 says, "Confess to one another therefore your faults [your slips, your false steps, your offenses, your sins] and [also for one another, that you may be healed] and restored [to a spiritual tone of mind and heart]. The earnest [heartfelt, continue] prayer of a righteous man makes tremendous power available [dynamic in its working]," (AMP). The above scripture gives the product a way to escape, but it requires confessing the sin. When the sin is not confessed, it is allowed to grow and expand. Therefore, everything is impacted by that sin. Confessing removes the root and the cleansing begins. A search of the history of this nation does not reveal an acknowledgment of her sin; the sin continued to grow and the generation after my father's generation continued to suffer the consequences of those sins.

In essence, the new changes brought a false hope. A hope that signified the nation was healing from its past and we were becoming a land where equality was for all. The outside changes were prominent and possible. The saying was if you could imagine it, you could become it. There were more blacks going to college, seeking degrees to become doctors, lawyers and other prestigious careers. The family's direction was becoming focused on acquiring things that once seemed out of reach. They were more cars on the road driven by people of color. Women of color fashion flourished, as they were able to buy goods from the local department stores. The family focus was bent on acquiring, instead of maintaining the identity that kept them together. Although, with the new changes came a sense of identity—it was based on a false conception. The new identity allowed progression to take place; however, progression for "real" change remained the same. The men of my father's generation embraced the changes along with everyone else, but they knew that change without a change of heart was not the best for the nation. The heart of many welcomed the increase in monetary gain, prosperity, yet their stance was still the same. Their mentality was of a superior posture. The men of my father's generation saw the deception. Their wisdom came from their Source. The heart of the nation didn't change. The seed was still there. They forewarned the people, yet their warning was futile; the change was imminent. However, they saw that change was only good if we kept our mind on the Source.

Chapter Ten

Freedom in My Father's Generation

The men of my father's generation recognized that the confession of sin was not high on the agenda of the founders, the church or the leaders of the land. This requirement by God was not received by the masses, "the authority of the people." This speaks volumes of the condition of the heart of those in leadership. It says that either they have not sinned, or that they don't recognize the sin. The scripture calls this deception. The heart has to be changed so that the heavenly Father can be known. Jeremiah 24:7 says, "And I will give them a heart to know [recognize, understand, and be acquainted with] Me, that I am the Lord; and they will be My people, and I will be their God, for they will return to Me with their whole heart," (AMP). The men of my father's generation recognized that as long as the heart remained corrupt, the nation could never truly know Him. Their prayers were that the eyes of the nation's understanding would be open to see what they had not seen and to hear what they had not heard, and to be what they had not been. They wanted the true meaning of "One nation under God" lived out in a nation whereby Christianity was a lifestyle modeled after Jesus Christ, not just empty words spoken by individuals.

The men of my father's generation recognized that the true measure of a Christian nation was its total commitment to the Lord Jesus Christ and His principles. This truth had to rise above the dysfunctional environment that had dominated the nation from the outset, which was a portion of its citizens lacked freedom that they were promised as a citizen of this nation. Freedom was a word that was not familiar to a segment of the population. As previously stated, freedom requires one to take responsibility and to be committed.

The essence of freedom is something that has to be learned. This means that the total package of freedom requires godly knowledge because the product has no concept of what true freedom is in the state of bondage. Remember, a "freedom cry" was heard from the outset of the country. The founders sought to establish a system that provided true freedom. Freedom was the number one objective that motivated the founders to come to the new country. True freedom goes beyond removing legal barriers.

True freedom is a process whereby the product has been totally emancipated through spirit, soul and body. Freedom to think is based on truth from the source of God rather than truth based on the concepts of the product. The renewing of the mind was essential in obtaining total freedom, yet the founders sought to establish this freedom through laws that focused on the outside rather than the condition of the heart. This challenge has plagued this nation, and she has not been able to overcome this challenge. It is with us today. This dysfunctional environment prevented them from recognizing the objective of the power of darkness. Thus, they were able only to react instead of taking responsibility. This is why praying was a high priority for the men of my father's generation.
They understood that true freedom was the result of having a personal relationship with Jesus Christ and that freedom as expressed by man is limited. Truth is the only means that brings total freedom (John 8: 31-32, and 36).

The will to achieve in my father's generation required something that the product didn't have. The answer was in the Lord Jesus. He has to become the number one priority. As long as the number one priority was "the authority of the people," the Lord Jesus would always be second. This meant that He was not valuable and that something else was more important than Him. Under these conditions, religion took His place as the number one priority.

Men of My Father's Generation

Thus, everyone was oppressed. Bondage had achieved her objective. The men of my father's generation recognized the traits of this bondage. 2 Peter 2:19 says, "They promise them liberty, when they themselves are slaves of depravity and defilement for by whatever anyone is made inferior or worse or is overcome, to that [person or thing] he is enslaved," (AMP). Those that sought to give freedom were also the servants of bondage and darkness. Bondage and darkness cannot produce life and freedom. The dog has been chasing his tail to no avail. The men of my father's generation made a decision, then, to choose life and freedom for themselves and the generations to come by standing and abiding in the Word.

Faith was the essential element that leveled the playing field. Faith rode on the back of hope, and became the reality by which they lived their lives. Throughout the Bible, faith was the means; while grace made the promises avail, faith gave them access. Faith confirmed what had not been revealed to the senses. Hebrews 11:1 says, "Now faith is the assurance [the confirmation, the title deed] of the things [we] hope for, being the proof of things [we] do not see and the conviction of their reality [faith perceiving as real fact what is not revealed to the senses]," (AMP). The men of my father's generation believed in the Word and allowed the Word to shape their perspective. The track record of faith has longevity throughout the history of the product; therefore, the men of my father's generation focused their attention on walking by faith and not by sight. Faith gave them access into a reality that was superior to the reality of the world. Faith made them aware that they were just as valuable to Him as others, and they were made in His image and after His likeness. Faith refuted the status quo, religion, tradition and "the authority of the people" because "the authority of people" was an inferior concept based on the inferior heart of those that supported it. Faith made itself available to all that would embrace it. The fingerprint of faith is all over the creation because God operates on faith. Genesis 1:2-3 says, "The earth was without form and an empty waste, darkness was upon the face of the very great deep. The Spirit of God was moving [hovering, brooding] over the face of the waters. And God said, let there be light: and there was light," (AMP).

It was faith that produced the light because faith is one of the characteristics of God. His kingdom was created and exists because of faith. The fingerprints of faith can be seen throughout the history of the world. It was faith in the Father, the Son, and the Holy Spirit that motivated my father's generation. Faith began where the will and knowledge of His word were known. Faith shifted the focus from what was seen with the natural eye to a picture that was seen through the spiritual eye. Faith created a picture, and the focus was on the creditability of the One that promised the picture. The men of my father's generation placed greater emphasis on the picture because they knew that faith was the confirmation of what they saw in the picture. Faith gave them the ability and equipped them for their assignment with strength and confidence. Faith enabled them to endure hardship, pain, shame, and disrespect. It says in 2 Corinthians 4:17-18, "For our light, momentary affliction [this slight distress of the passing hour] is ever more and more abundantly preparing and [producing and achieving for us an everlasting weight of glory [beyond all measure, excessively surpassing all comparisons and calculations, a vast and transcendent glory and blessedness never to cease!]. Since we consider and look not to the things that are seen but to things that are unseen; for the things that are visible are temporal [brief and fleeting], but the things that are invisible are deathless and everlasting," (AMP). Only by faith in the Author and the Finisher (Jesus) were they able to stand, and having done all, to still stand. The very characteristics of faith are so far reaching, so invincible and invigorating that the natural mind is not able to comprehend it. The men of my father's generation reached beyond the natural. Faith reaches into the realm of the spirit. Faith gives life to that which was dead and produces a marriage between the spirit realm and the natural realm. What is seen in the natural yielded to the superiority of the spirit realm.

When the will of the Father is known through His Word, and it is believed, faith takes that belief and invigorates it with life and energy. Faith in Jesus Christ is the only means by which one can be saved. Throughout history, faith has played a vital role in the survival of families. It was the faith of Abraham when he was willing to give up his son, set a precedent in earth whereby the Father gave up His Only Son. The true depth of faith is still being established. The challenge for a segment of the church is that the faith message has been predominantly focused on concerns, sicknesses and needs. Faith gives the believer access to Power. Faith empowered the believer. Faith gives the believer access to authority. The same grace through faith that brought salvation to humanity has also given the believer the ability to walk in authority and exercise power. It is in this area that a segment of the church has failed to include the power and authority as a benefit that all believers have.

Every challenge that this nation has faced was an opportunity for the church to exercise the power that has been given to her. At the outset, the founders had an opportunity to exercise the power, but they chose to place more value in "the authority of the people" than the power of His Word. They chose to seek the wisdom and knowledge of the people rather than the wisdom and knowledge of God. This action established where their heart was. Their heart had more confidence in the people than the Creator. This action opened the door to pride, and that door has never been shut. It was pride that declared that people of color were less than whites. This pride was in violation of His word: Isaiah 42:8 says, "I am the Lord; that is My name! And My glory I will not give to another, nor My praise to graven images," (AMP). Rejecting His principles while embracing the principles of the people opened the door to idolatry and all of its family members. This spirit is not easy to identify. It is subtle and works behind the scene, but remember, the prophet Isaiah got access to record in heaven when he wrote, "And My glory I will not give to another" (Isaiah 42:8). Glory is the essence of a thing. When God's glory is removed, His presence is removed. When His presence is removed, the enemy has total access, and the emphasis will be placed on good things from a natural perspective, but not righteous things based on His word. The devastation of the Civil War was the result of failing to place a high priority on His Word while magnifying the concept of "the authority of the people."

Frustration

When truth is rejected, lies rule with impunity, darkness has total control, and the nation and its people suffer. This suffering is passed on to generation after generation. Remember, when His glory is removed, it removes His power and His authority. Thus, the product has no supporting foundation and everything he touches is vile, polluted, and contaminated. This means his best effort falls short of reaching its objective because the mind has the will, but the heart does not have commitment. The focus is on good intentions, but not righteous intentions, meaning that good intentions are inferior to righteous intentions. The men of my father's generation recognized that good was not sufficient. The things that were good in the sight of the product were evil in the sight of God because He sees the end before He creates the product. The founders of this nation were not wise enough to see the end; therefore, what they perceived as good to natural eyes was, in fact, evil, vile, and polluted.

Again, the men of my father's generation had to discipline themselves to think, reason, and see themselves as it is written in the word. Becoming frustrated was a great challenge for them. The

Men of My Father's Generation

opportunity for frustration was always present. The objective of frustration is to invalidate the power of His Grace, and an aspect of the church played on this team by remaining silent. Because the roots of deception were rooted and grounded so deeply in the thinking of the nation, a lie became the truth, and the church brought credibility to the lie. This lie magnified the product, "the authority of the people," while minimizing the finished work of the Lord Jesus. This action produced a spirit of confusion, an erroneous picture of the truth, and the lie was expanded. Truth had to substantiate daily, because there was an ongoing effort by the power of darkness that gave the lie the right to identify the men of my father's generation. They were belittled and reduced to subhuman, meaning that they didn't deserve the same treatment as others. The subhuman mentality produced a spirit that rejected all forms of responsibility. These traits are the products of evil spirits that were at work then as well as now with the objective of stealing, killing and destroying. Thankfully, my father's generation recognized these faults and refused to accept them as truth.

Again, truth, faith, grace and commitment had to work in unison to overcome the obstacles of lies, darkness, fear and a lack of knowledge. Lies had such a stronghold that lies became the reality that most lived. The lies took root and spread its venom into their consciences to such a degree that truth could not be recognized through natural means. Darkness ruled with impunity, and fear piggybacked on this lie to such a degree that fear became the norm: fear of one group losing its position, fear that the oppressed would become the oppressors, fear to teach the oppressed to read because knowledge would place a demand on freedom, and more. Thus, the greatest enemy to bondage was knowledge.

Keeping the men of my father's generation in bondage would bring credibility to the notion that the oppressed was created to service the oppressor. Remember, the objective was to keep the oppressed thinking that they were an after-thought, although they were part of the first creation. The thinking and reasoning of the generation became an asset then. Proverbs 23:7 says, "For as he thinks in his heart, so is he," (AMP). This was a critical element of the enemy's plan. The leaders wanted to keep the men of my father's generation thinking and reasoning in a negative way about themselves. They wanted to keep them thinking and reasoning that they were an after-thought. The men of my father's generation had to place the truth of the Word above religion and tradition. The truth of The Word of God had to identify them; they had to allow the Holy Spirit to dismantle all the erroneous information that had been stored over generations. They had to repudiate things that were held with high esteem by the masses. The Word of the God had to take precedence over the status quo.

What a challenge this must have been for them to evaluate everything they had been taught, yet still give the Holy Spirit the opportunity to become a filter, wedging out that which was not profitable, that which didn't identify them! The truth had to become their objective. Proverbs 23:23 says, "Buy the truth and sell it not; not only that, but also get discernment and judgment, instruction and understanding," (AMP). They went after truth with all their heart. Truth was as important as breathing. Just as breathing is essential to living, truth is essential to life. Truth is essential to freedom and productivity. Other essential elements of this journey were the ability to discern, to evaluate, and to make sound decisions based on truth. Truth gives access to wisdom and knowledge. To reiterate, the knowledge of truth corrected the impaired vision so that they could see themselves as He saw them. It also changed their perspective and their reality. Their knowledge of truth elevated their views and impacted the other generations. Truth brought stability and confidence. Truth placed a demand on responsibility. Truth enabled them to recognize that they had been taken by both political parties. Neither side was willing to deal with the issue of racism. (We must remember that the northern states at one time enjoyed the benefits of slavery.) The fact is, neither side woke up one morning and said. "We are complying with the Constitution. The 13th, 14th, and 15th Amendments are not being enforced." Therefore, neither party had anything to boast about. Today, nothing has changed. Conservatives and Liberals are in the same box as it relates to dealing with the issue of race. This is one area where the two parties share in not taking responsibility, and not complying with their laws.

Freedom was documented on paper to reflect the nation's stance or ideology; yet, it was not her reality. The freedom that was documented did not reflect or represent the masses; it did not represent the men of my father's generation. The freedom that was documented into words were beautifully written, but tragically denounced. True freedom couldn't be given by a corrupt vessel, but a perfect vessel. They were free, not because of a document, but because their Source set them free. "So if the Son liberates you [makes you free men], then you are really and unquestionably free," John 8:36 (AMP).

Chapter Eleven
Moving Forward in My Father's Generation

In many cases, the black vote has become a football used by both political sides. Politicians place greater emphasis on other things than on the issue of race. The history of the nation has been to react and not take responsibility. When a major event takes place whereby it is known around the world, the pattern of the nation has been to react by addressing the fruit and not the root. This pattern dates back before the Civil War, whereby truth was forsaken for the "authority of the people." Those that allowed the status quo to identify them produced sons and daughters who, today, are struggling to discover their true identity. Fathers are still abandoning their children because they were not taught about taking responsibility. Children are growing up and being controlled and dominated by what others are say. It's obvious that there is a deficit in the earth for leadership in the home.

The nation must acknowledge that this enemy is not flesh and blood. Because of this lack of knowledge, each side points a finger at the other while the enemy eats the lunch of the northerners and the southerners as he did the slaves and their offsprings. The men of my father's generation were the fruit of that wicked seed that impacted all that had a lack of knowledge. Thankfully, these men knew that the most important thing for them was to obtain knowledge. The sources that brought conviction and strengthened the root were tradition and religion; they controlled the way of thinking and reasoning. Since religion and tradition master the art of unity, they ruled with impunity. However, the people didn't make the earth, nor did the people create themselves. Therefore, if the product is going to be successful, the Source that made him must be the foundation by which everything is established. God is superior to the product. Let me reiterate, Isaiah 55:8-11 says, "For My thoughts are not your thoughts, neither are your ways My ways, says the Lord. For as the heavens are higher than the earth, so are My ways higher than your ways, and My thoughts than your thoughts. For as the rain and snow come down from heavens, and return not there again, but water the earth and make it bring forth and sprout, that it may give seed to the sower and bread to the eater. So shall My word be that goes forth out of My mouth: it shall not return to Me void [without producing any effect, useless], but it shall accomplish that which I please and purpose, and it shall prosper in the things for which I sent it," (AMP). Only the Creator of this world could make such a bold and broad statement. Therefore, the words and laws promulgated by the product are useless without any effect because the product doesn't possess the ability to carry it out.

The actions of the majority in no way protected the country from darkness, corruption or greed. The heart determines the action. This does not mean the founders were evil. It means that they possibly controlled by the desire to create a masterpiece when, in fact; they were not qualified to do so. Proverbs 3:6-7 says, "In all your ways know, recognize and acknowledge Him, and He will direct and make straight and plain your paths. Be not wise in your own eyes; reverently fear and worship the Lord and turn [entirely] away from evil," (AMP). The first requirement is to recognize Him, His authority, His wisdom, His knowledge, and His love. The result is that He will direct and make the paths straight. If He is not acknowledged, He is not obligated to direct the path. Acknowledging Him is more than words only. It means to reverence and worship Him, esteeming Him, always keeping Him the top priority in one's life. When the opinions of the majority are preferred over His words, it means that the majority is favored over Him. This single act opens the door to other negative things, because it

Men of My Father's Generation

shows we are worshiping the creature over the Creator.

The courageous men of my father's generation had to monitor their hearts daily by refusing to buy into the lie that they were somehow inferior to others. This required great discipline, balance, and the leading of the Holy Spirit. It also required the repudiation of self by placing things in their proper perspective, in the Father, the Son, and the Holy Spirit. It placed a demand on them to think according to the Word, and only the Word provided their identification. The incredible act of these men speaks volumes to their determination to overcome what others saw as a liability. They wanted to make it into something positive. The driving force was their faith in the Lord Jesus, and their desire to take a negative and make it into a positive. They refused to allow the circumstances to steal their joy. James 1:2-4 says, "Consider it wholly joyful, my brethren, whenever you are enveloped in or encounter trials of any sort or fall into various temptations. Be assured and understand that the trial and proving of your faith bring out endurance, steadfastness and patience. But let endurance and steadfastness and patience have full play and do a thorough work, so that you may be [people] perfectly and fully developed [with no defects], lacking nothing (AMP). Remember, they had to consider it or count it as joy. This required more than lip service. It required a heart that placed all of its trust in the Lord.

The strength of faith is wisdom and knowledge. Wisdom must take root in the heart, and knowledge must have a love affair with all aspects of the soul: mind, will, emotion, imagination, and intellect. This releases an understanding that is beyond the natural comprehension that provokes faith. This level of faith was where the men of my father's generation rested and placed their total confidence. They have faith in God based on His written word because faith began where the will of the Father is known. Faith is sustained when there is joy because the joy of the Lord produces much strength. These men maintained an attitude of joy. Joy was essential if they were to overcome the challenge that they faced. This level of joy looked beyond the natural environment, focused on the unseen, and came from a personal relationship with the Lord Jesus Christ. His joy became their joy as they looked to Him. Hebrews 12:2-3 says, "Looking away [from all that will distract] to Jesus, Who is the Leader and Source of our faith [giving the first incentive for our belief] and is also its Finisher [bringing it to maturity and perfection]. He, for the joy [of obtaining the prize] that was set before Him, endured the cross, despising and ignoring the shame and is now seated at the right hand of the throne of God. Just think of Him, Who endured from sinners such grievous opposition and bitter hostility against Himself [reckon up and consider it all in comparison with your trials], so that you may not grow weary or exhausted, losing heart and relaxing and fainting in your minds," (AMP). These scriptures became the foundational scripture on which they stood. The focus had to be on Jesus Christ, who knew no sin, but instead suffered the consequences of sin for all humanity.

Looking to Jesus Christ produced a joy that far exceeded their tribulations, disappointment and shame. It far exceeded the name calling, the fact that they were looked upon as inferior, and a byword. As a result, when times got extremely hard, they would go and read these scriptures, and the words brought comfort. Jesus said in John 6:63, "It is the Spirit Who gives life [He is the Life-giver]; the flesh conveys no benefit whatever [there is no profit in it], the words [truths] that I have been speaking to you are spirit and life," (AMP). They recognized that the real life was not in the natural things, but the true life was in abiding in His word. They also recognized that the true measure of their life on earth would not be measured in longevity but in substance; not in quantity, but in quality. A standard that represents Him in all aspects for humanity, they suffered and stood in the gap for the nation. They saw their struggle as an opportunity to represent the Lord Jesus by praying for those whose eyes were blinded from the truth, by living a life whereby those that were oppressing would see the life of Jesus Christ in them.

Their faithfulness to the Lord Jesus gave them access and opportunity to pray for those in authority, to love their enemies, to do good to those that abused them. In doing so, the eyes of many of those that had negative views changed. Many of those that were oppressed came to know Jesus and accepted Him as their Savior and Lord. And while in the natural it looked as if it was all in vain, the inner man was renewed day by day. The stronger the opposition was, the more their strength was equal to the task. This was the result of a mindset that was constantly renewed. The external things didn't change the mindset. This lifestyle gave them access to wisdom and knowledge that enabled them to accomplish the impossible. Their natural skills confounded those that opposed them, and their spiritual insight placed them in a position to reveal truth to the very individuals that looked on them with contempt.

Change over Time

The attitude of separation was always on the mind of many. This was another lie that had to be addressed, and it was addressed by declaring what the Bible says in Galatians 3:28, "There is [now no distinction] neither Jew nor Greek, there is neither slave nor free, there is not male and female; for you are all one in Christ Jesus," (AMP). The concept of separation is a product religion based on the ideas and opinions of the product and not the words of God. This means that religion has driven this nation and not Christianity. The notion that this is a Christian nation no longer stands. The men of my father's generation recognized this disparity, and they chose to place their confidence in the Lord Jesus.

Placing confidence in the Lord Jesus put them at odds with the status quo, but they maintained their position. They were mindful of the credibility of His word, the leading of the Holy Spirit, and His promise of never leaving them alone. In many respects, the adversity that they faced motivated them even more to press harder for themselves as well as future generations. They allowed responsibility to place a high demand on them. This demand said they would never give up, give in, or give out. Pleasing the Father was more important to them than living in pleasure. In many cases, they felt driven by a higher power and this power was the Holy Spirit that guided them into all truth. The truth revealed that God wanted His sons and daughters to fellowship as one of Jesus Christ revealed this truth in John 17:11, 20-21: "And [now] I am no more I the world, but these are [still] in the world, and I am coming to You, Holy Father, keep in Your Name [in the knowledge of Yourself] those whom You have given Me, that they may be one as We][are one]. Neither for these alone do I pray [it is not for their sake only that I make this request], but also for all those who will ever come to believe in [trust in, cling to, rely on] Me through their word and teaching. That they all may be one, [just] as You, Father, are in Me and I in You, that they also may be one in Us, so that the world may believe and be convinced that You have sent Me," (AMP).

The men of my father's generation were convinced that disunity was the result of rejecting the teaching of the Lord Jesus. When He is removed from the table, the product no longer has access to the Father; therefore, the product will always malfunction. The malfunction is the result of a lack of knowledge. When a natural product is not complying according to the manual, the result is a malfunction. When the product created in the image and likeness of the Manufacturer (God) failed to comply with His directive, the result is a meltdown and a malfunction. Adam rejected truth, and the result was separation. The rejecting of truth disconnected

Men of My Father's Generation

Adam from the Source, and in Adam's unholy state, he gave the enemy total access to the product. Jesus came to restore the product back to God, the Father. When He is rejected, the product remains adrift, driven by the winds of darkness. Therefore, the product is not able to function properly, and his best intentions cannot be achieved because he is competing against a spirit that can only be defeated by the finished work of the Lord Jesus.

The founders and their best intentions for a nation of freedom were not committed to nor did they have the ability to carry their intentions out. Commitment was to be sustained with truth, and intimacy with truth is the only means by which total freedom can be achieved. Knowing the truth sets one free. The truth that was needed in order to obtain freedom was abiding in the principles of the Lord Jesus. He fulfilled the requirement; He became the flesh so that through Him total freedom was available. The limited freedom that the laws by the founders promulgated fell short of meeting the requirement. Meeting the requirement required everyone to be connected to the Lord Jesus.

After the Emancipation, these men, in their short time of benefiting from some measure of freedom, recognized a decline in love, righteousness, and respect not only from those in charge, but the total environment. They would often discuss how things had changed as they grew from childhood to adulthood. The changes that were obvious to them were a lack of respect displayed by all, and a breakdown in the family of the former slaves, as well as the former slave owners. They observed that the former slaves, as well as the former slave owners shared these common traits: a lack of respect and greed. These traits appeared to be expressed by a vast majority. The owners of the farms and the companies that they worked for were taking advantage of family members, which resulted in, the workers who worked on the farm and in these companies did the same. Brothers began taking advantage of brothers. 2 Timothy 3:1-3 says, "But understand this, that in the last days will come [set in] perilous times of great stress and trouble [hard to deal with and hard to bear]. For people will be lovers of self and [utterly] self-centered, lovers of money and aroused by an inordinate [greedy] desire for wealth, proud and arrogant and contemptuous boasters. They will be abusive [blasphemous, scoffing, disobedient to parents, ungrateful, unholy and profane. [They will be] without natural [human] affection [callous and inhuman], relentless [admitting of no truce or appeasement]; [they will be] slanders [false accusers, troublemakers] intemperate and loose in morals and conduct, uncontrolled and fierce, haters of good," (AMP).

The fathers of the men of my father's generation would say these traits were demonstrated when they were children; therefore, they were not a new phenomenon. In the slavery environment, they were expressed. There were lovers of self and were taking advantage of the slaves as well as others, and there was a greater desire for wealth than a relationship with the Lord Jesus Christ. People even exploited the poor whites and disregarded the works of the Lord Jesus daily; and yet, maintained their positions in the local church. Many were without natural affection and saw others as inhuman. They insisted on maintaining the same spirit that provoked the Civil War. Many expressed no remorse for their action, and the spirit of being lovers of themselves controlled the thinking of the former slaves as well as the former slave owners. This selfish mentality grew by leaps and bounds- the person that had plenty and the person that had nothing. The Bible is very clear about what was going on in the beginning of the last days. In essence, the Civil War was an indication that the last days had arrived, but no one took notice.

The times themselves motivated the men of my father's generation to renew their minds daily, to take up their cross and follow Jesus.

Men of My Father's Generation

They had an incentive to go forward, to stand, to impact the next generation with truth, wisdom, knowledge, and understanding. They had an incentive to take responsibility and not to react, to use godly wisdom and not the limited knowledge of this world. They made a decision that all the challenges that they face also presented opportunity. 2 Corinthians 4:8-11 says, "We are afflicted in every way, but not crushed; perplexed, but not despairing. Persecuted, but not forsaken: struck down, but not destroyed. Always carrying about in the body the dying of Jesus, so that the life of Jesus also may be manifested in our body. For we who live are constantly being delivered over to death for Jesus' sake, so that the life of Jesus also may be manifested in our mortal flesh," (NAS). This life whereby they chose to live for Him gave them extreme abilities, wisdom, knowledge, and understanding that didn't come from man. They tapped into power, wisdom, knowledge and understanding of the Holy Spirit. This insight sustained them. Their strongest desire was to please Him, and the reward for that desire was that His peace rested on them. The Holy Spirit guided them into truth that was not available to others that had greater learning in the world's system. The knowledge of the world is inferior to His knowledge.

Proverbs 2:9-11 says, "Then you will understand righteousness, justice, and fair dealing [in every area and relation]; yes, you will understand every good path. For skillful and godly wisdom shall enter into your heart, and knowledge shall be pleasant to you. Discretion shall watch over you, and understanding shall keep you," (AMP). This means that justice and fair dealing cannot comprehend abiding in the arena of man's wisdom, for fair dealing is beyond the ability of the natural man. The wisdom of the One that created the product must take root in the heart. This wisdom must be accessed by faith. The five departments of the soul that we discussed earlier must be embraced and have a love affair with knowledge. The godly knowledge far exceeds the knowledge of the product. Discretion gave my father the ability to make wise choices. His understanding became a device that protected him in all his ways.

The learning skills my father accumulated enabled him to read, but godly wisdom, knowledge and understanding rested on him as a result of asking and being filled with the Holy Spirit. James 1:5 says, "If any of you is deficient in wisdom, let him ask of the giving God [Who gives] to everyone liberally and ungrudgingly, without reproaching or faultfinding, and it will be given him," (AMP). The conditions that they were living in provoked them to ask for wisdom because they knew that the limited wisdom and knowledge of the world were not sufficient for them. The action of the enemy and the *"powers that be"* required wisdom, knowledge and understanding beyond the natural. He was able to confuse those supposedly over him with his wisdom, knowledge and understanding. I know for a fact that the owner of the farm that we lived on would seek my dad's wisdom in making decisions. This was not an isolated case. Many would seek the wisdom from the senior black men in the community. Everybody called these men "uncles." Many Sundays, our front yard would be filled with blacks as well as whites seeking information from my father about jobs. The spiritual knowledge of my father enabled him to go out and obtain jobs in the area of building, and these men would seek employment from him. He didn't see his talents as making him better than them. He saw it as an opportunity to be a blessing to others. It is this attitude that made these men special in their generation; it also gave them the desire to show others that listened to them that giving and serving were important. Obedience brings a benefit that money cannot buy. It also opens doors that earthly knowledge could not open. These men left a legacy that was more valuable than gold, rubies, or silver.

They maintained a positive attitude at all times. They were mindful that the battle was not their battle. Jesus already paid the ultimate price for their victory. They had concluded that it was their responsibility to live out what He had provided. This attitude gave them courage, confidence, and strength to live in an environment that constantly put them down and looked on them as inferior. They were forced to renew their minds daily. They were forced to place the principles of the Lord Jesus above every challenge. They chose to maintain a conviction whereby they lived each day looking to Jesus. He was not only their Savior and Lord, but He was the Author of their faith. Hebrews 12:2 says, "Looking away [from all that will distract] to Jesus, Who is the Leader and the Source of our faith [giving the first incentive for our belief] and is also its Finisher [bringing it to maturity and perfection]. He, for the joy [of obtaining the prize] that was set before Him, endured the cross, despising and ignoring the shame, and is now seated at the right hand of the throne of God," (AMP).

This revelation of truth sustained them night and day. When they faced negative situations or enormous obstacles, they were not moved. Their confidence in the Lord Jesus gave them strength, and their joy was compromised even when it was impossible in the natural. The natural man could not comprehend the totality of what they went through. When a citizen is rejected by his own government and the source of light - the church - embraces the government, this situation does not give the citizen many options. The natural response is hatred and bitterness; however, the love of Jesus Christ gave them another option. As reprehensible as it was, love covered all sins and love fulfilled the will and principles of the Lord Jesus Christ. This love enabled them to move forward.

Chapter Twelve
The Hope of My Father's Generation to the Next Generation

Most of these incredible men have died, but they left a legacy that speaks volume of their relationship with the Lord Jesus. They place the finished work of the Lord Jesus above their circumstances, above the status quo, and above race. They displayed the highest level of the Agape love complying with the commandment of walking in love and seeing the best of their fellowman, John 13:35," By this shall all [men]know that you are My disciples, if you love one another [if you keep on showing love among yourselves," (AMP). Love was the motivator for taking responsibility for their families, emphasizing the importance of good work ethics. Love was the motivator for encouraging others to do likewise, maximizing the gifts that were in them. This level of love rose to the level of standing on the teaching of the Lord Jesus even when opposition was extremely great. This level of love provoked them to love their enemies and those that persecuted them. This level of love provoked them to see opportunity where the masses saw obstacles. This level of love provoked them to challenge the status quo, resulting in whites and blacks working together in total unity.

The Jernigan family stands out among all the families that represented this love during that period in time. Their love was beyond understanding. Just recently the granddaughter of Mr. Jim Jernigan stated that she always thought we were members of their family. The foundation for their level of love was the Lord Jesus Christ, the focus was on Him. The love of the Lord places a demand on taking responsibility, seeing others through His eyes.

Mindful of His unconditional love for all races creed or color because we were made in His image and after His likeness. The love that the heavenly Father instill in them was the result of Father displaying His love by sending His son, 1 John 10-11 [Amp] "In this is love: not that we loved God, but that He loved us and sent His Son to be propitiation [the atoning sacrifice] for our sins. Beloved, if God loved us so [very much], we also ought to love one another." Notice the command is to love one another and the one another consist of individuals from other ethnic groups.

These courageous men epitomize this level of love. The few that remain still displays this level of love: Pa Pierce, Mr. James Miller, Mr. Wes Brunson and many more. The late Mr. Loran Smith was another man of my father's generation who impacted his children and his community in an exemplary manner. His son, Chief Master Sergeant Loran Smith Jr., now retired from the Air Force was a second generation of the Tuskegee Airmen. Chief Master Sergeant Loran not only put his life on the line protecting the country, but he and others put their life on the line during the Montgomery boycott by providing transportation for those that boycotted the city buses. His father was a man of wisdom, who focused on the finished work of the Lord Jesus. His fatherly love and his willingness to teach his children had enormous impact on Retired Chief Master Sergeant Loran. He was one of the most decorated enlisted personnel in the Aerospace Physiological Training career field. He was the first of his race in this field, and foundation was lay by his father, a man of my father's generation. The environment that Mr. Loran Smith Sr. established was profound in producing light where there was darkness. It produced truth in the midst of blindness. Two of the most valuable traits that Mr. Loran Smith Sr. left his children were taking responsibilities, and seeing opportunities where others saw obstacles.

Pa Pierce, who is three years younger than my dad, is also a man of

Men of My Father's Generation

my father's generation that demonstrates and displays the love of the Lord. His love remains steadfast despite the condition he was forced to live under less than a second class citizen. His love for others including this nation was never compromised. His love for the heavenly Father and the finished of the Lord Jesus is unwavering. The wisdom that he displays is worth more than gold, and this wisdom is the result of having a personal relationship with the Lord Jesus. This man has incredible knowledge that the world needs- a lesson of steadfastness, courage and dedication. These men loved their family, and the nation, and they paid the ultimate price. Pa Pierce gives all the glory and praise to the Lord Jesus for His unconditional love. Romans 5:8 says, "But God shows and clearly proves His [own] love for us by the fact that while we were still sinners, Christ [the Messiah, the Anointed One] died for us," (AMP). The traits that Pa Pierce displays provoke me to call him dad; the likeness of my dad is unparalleled. He is still a man on a mission to display the love of the Lord Jesus, to provoke others to maximizing their potential, released their God given purpose, and to be successful despite the condition.

These men managed their emotions when someone was constantly saying something that was irritating and provoking. They were extremely patient. Proverbs 16:32, "He who is slow to anger is better than the mighty, he who rules his [own] spirit than he who takes a city," (AMP). Pa Pierce demonstrated the highest level of endurance and love. At the age of ninety his love walk has not waver nor has his desire to instill in others the art of taking responsibility. Responsibility places a demand on manhood; responsibility denotes the ability to respond to the situation, whether positive or negative. Pa Pierce took on responsibility from a child and it has grown in every area of his life. Because he loved taking on responsibility, the heavenly Father used him mightily in instilling these same traits in his children and grandchildren. He and my father had many things in common, but one thing that stands out, they grew up without natural father. The positive aspect of this was that they were greatly influence by individuals that knew the value of taking on responsibility. Pa Pierce tells the story of when he arrived in Detroit he stayed with an older couple and the man treated him as if he was his biological son. The knowledge that he received from him was priceless.

Others that played a vital role in men of my father's generation beside those already mention is my cousin, William Taylor, Deacon James D. Curry, Mr. Charley Health, Mr. O.B. Smith, just to mention a few. Although they are all deceased, they left a profound legacy that this nation needs. A legacy of taking on responsibility, a legacy that sees taking on responsibility as an opportunity. Cousin William Taylor was a man of responsibility, and he instills the same traits in his children. Deacon James D. Curry played a vital role in mentoring my dad. They worked together. The last two names, Mr. Charley Heath and O.B. Smith were Caucasian men who demonstrated a level of wisdom and love that exceeded far beyond the norm. They took on the responsibility of respecting individuals of color when it was not the popular thing to do. They challenged the status quo. What was unique about these men is that they took on the responsibility of teaching their children, as well as grandchildren to respect and love others not just those of their ethnicity. They left the legacy of leading by setting an example, challenging the status quo, and being the leaders God created them to be. They refused to allow the rejection by others to determine their true identity. John 1:11, "He came to that which belonged to Him [to His own, His domain, creation, things world], and they who were His own did not receive Him and did not welcome Him," (AMP). These great men affected changes and their dedication along with prayer impacted a nation.

When you trace the roots of the Civil Right Movement, you will discover that prayer and courageous leadership played a vital role.

Men of My Father's Generation

The power of prayer is obvious. 2 Chronicles 7:14 says, "If My people, who are called by My name, shall humble themselves, pray, seek, crave, and require of necessity My face and turn from their wicked ways, then will I hear from heaven, forgive their sin, and heal their land," (AMP). Notice, the healing of the land does not come from laws promulgated by the creature. The healing of the land comes from prayer. These men sought, craved and had an intimate relationship with the Son. This intimacy along with prayer produced a level of freedom that could not be legislated by man. Jeremiah 31:33, "I will put my law in their minds and write it on their hearts. I will be their God and they will be my people," (Leadership Bible). These men were greatly influenced by the word of the Lord. His words were placed above the laws of man. While their prayers brought on changes, they knew that true changes would only be manifested when the heart was changed. As a result many of these men stood in gap, for the church, as well as the nation. The stand that they took required them to be doers of the word and not hearers only. They refused to allow the status quo to take priority over the finished work of the Lord Jesus. They places great emphasis on accepting responsibility, seeing taking responsibility as a huge access and that wouldimpact the next generation in a positive way. Mr. Charley Health is a prime example of teaching your children and grandchildren to honor and respect others. I recent saw his grandson and he displayed the same traits as his grandfather in showing respect and honor to older people of all ethnicity. These men were driven by a passion to please the Lord Jesus. They placed pleasing Him as their number one objective.

Their personal sacrifices were enormous because they knew that the responsibility placed on them demanded sacrifice. Accomplishing the assignment took priority over the personal sacrifices. They obtained fulfillment from the success of others. Dr. Nathan Hodges indicated to me that my dad encouraged him and as a result, he went on to become chancellor at a major university. He had personal view of character of these courageous men and it had lasting impression on him. He was an eye witness of how they handled the challenges and responsibilities that they accepted. The driven force of the Holy Spirit elevated them above the challenges of being perplexed and emotional overcome. They refused to allow the troubles of the challenge to impact them. 2 Corinthians 4:8-10] "We are troubled on every side, yet not distressed; we are perplexed, but not in despair. Persecuted, but not forsaken; cast down, but not destroyed. Always bearing about in the body the dying of the Lord Jesus, that the life also of Jesus might be made manifest in our body," (KJV).

The leadership that they displayed was priceless and should be taught in every college in this nation. The very nature of taking on this level of responsibility released criticism; the criticism was a test of their maturity and their incredible leadership. In many cases, the criticism came from the source that should have been their greatest strength the church. They refused to allow the opposition from the church to trouble them: Galatians 6:17] "From henceforth let no man trouble me; for I bear in my body the marks of the Lord Jesus," (KJV). These men maintained a positive perspective of life and they placed great value on accountability and responsibility. They saw accountability and responsibility as being synonymous with manhood. They refused to waver in their stand to project righteousness; every man listed in chapter displayed the true meaning of Christianity. Many confess their Christianity with words, but they demonstrated their faith with action. Their Christianity consists of partnership with Jesus Christ, He being the Head and they were the body. The body takes on a responsibility that has been expressed by the Head. Taking on responsibility is motivated by the Head because He took on the responsibility for the sins of humanity. Standing up for truth is the mark that measure true leadership and the traits of a true believer: John 8: 31-32,] "So Jesus said to those Jews who had believed in Him,

Men of My Father's Generation

if you abide in My word [hold fast to My teachings and live accordance with them], you are truly my disciples. And you will know the Truth, and the Truth will set you free," (AMP). These courageous men knew that true freedom was outside the ability of the creature, true freedom could only be achieved by having a personal relationship with the Lord Jesus.

This level of freedom consist of: spirit, soul and body, and it is available to all that put their trust in the Lord Jesus. These men were the giants of their day and they left a legacy that is deep and widerooted and grounded in truth. Heaven and earth will take the stand on their behalf and declare that they produced light doing a season of great darkness, truth in the midst of lies and deception, and commitment when others were kicking the can down the road. A time when the government expressed a positive view concerning all of its citizen, but failed to enforce its own laws. A time when a segment of the church allowed darkness to rule with impunity and the fruit of darkness became the reality. A time when an aspect of the church closed her eyes to the aborting of potential and purpose while these men saw value in each person. Every manufacturer knows that the purpose of his or her product is as valuable as the product. These men recognized this truth and they placed great value on encouraging all to release their God given potential and purpose. Yes, they recognized the heavenly Father had placed potential and purpose in everyone born in the earth from all ethnic groups. To prevent anyone from achieving his or her assignment impacts all and every ethnicity will suffered the lost.

The voices of these courageous men are calling out from the grave just as Abel's blood called out. The message to this generation of men take hold of responsibility and accountability, embrace responsibility as dear to life as breathing and accountability as the measure of true manhood. The voices are saying in order for this truth to becomes the reality the men of this generation must allow Jesus Christ to reveal their truth identity. The voices are saying, stop complaining and be totally committed. The voices are saying; see every challenge as an opportunity mindful of the finished work of the Lord. The voices are saying that the strength for such a task comes from Him: Philippians 4:13, "I have strength for all things in Christ Who empowers me [I am ready for anything and equal to anything through Him Who infuses inner strength into me; I am self-sufficient in Christ's sufficiency," (AMP) This level of commitment places a demand on being controlled by the wisdom of the Lord, and willingness to impact in a positive way the current and next generation.

Final Thoughts

It takes special men to build a country. While prominent great men were making their legacies with money, power, and prestige, building great corporations, massive railroads, prestigious universities, landmark bridges, and grandeur buildings, all significant in establishing a nation, there were special men, on the sidelines, often over-looked, and considered by many as unimportant, uneducated, and lowly in disposition, standing in the gap for the nation. These men, in their meek and humble demeanor, were not the norms in a setting that was portrayed, or stated the norm. These men took the works of Jesus Christ, the love of the Father to the levels they were intended. They didn't see racism, status quo, inferiority or superiority. They didn't see one being better than the other, nor did they see social classes, or color.

The men of my father's generation recognized that the great Physician was Jesus Christ, and He came to heal all sickness. 1 Corinthians 15:21-22 says, "For since [it was] through a man that death [came into the world, it is] also through a Man that the resurrection of the dead [has come]. For just as [because of their union of nature] in Adam all people die, so also [by virtue of their union of nature] shall all in Christ be made alive" [Amplified]. The men of my father's generation recognized their need for a Source greater than the product. Knowing this truth gave them a huge advantage as it relates to dealing with opposition and navigating through the challenging seas.

These men are not written about in our history books. Their legacies are not documented. They are forgotten about from the masses, and yet these unsung heroes were the men who stabilized the nation with their prayers, while others were building it. They didn't receive the recognition for their works. They endured the abuse, the prejudices, the degradation, and yes, the humiliation and denial to live freely in a country that profess equality to all. The men of my father's generation were men of honor, courage, black, white, and other ethnicities. They understood brotherhood, unity and love. They were their "brother's keeper." They didn't succumb to the lack of spiritual support from the church, or the lack of support from the government or nation as a whole. And while many fought in wars to protect the nation's freedom, even though they were not free, they were heroes- not because of a war, but because they endured the scars and wounds from everyday battle.

While we applaud and praise the men who built this nation, and marvel at their accomplishments, yearning to obtained half of what they did, we fail to see the special men who made a difference, who fought back, not with words, but with demonstrations of love, kindness, and humility. Men, who did not focus on legalistic observance, but were devoted to God's desires, and His Word. Men who took the scriptures literally, "Love your brother as you love yourself." Men, who prayed without ceasing, who raised their children in the abomination of the Lord, and often times were looked at as second-class citizens. Men who were color-blind, and only saw what God saw. Men who made a difference, changed laws, and were prepared to fight to the end to make that difference.

Yes, we praise, the rich and powerful men, after all, they built this great nation. However, without the men in my father's generation standing in the gap to sustain the nation, we would not be where we are today. If there was ever a book to read, Men of My father's Generation" is the one.
The Publisher

Foot Note

1. Lincoln, Abraham. Keynote Address: "House Divided Speech." Republican State Convention.
    Springfield, Illionois. June 16, 1858.

James Thornton

Author's Biography

James Thornton was born in a small town in lower Alabama. He is the son of a farmer. The discipline that he received from his father placed a demand on him to impact others. He served his country in the navy and the army. It was in the navy where he met his lovely wife, Nathalee, of forty-six years. They have four children, and six grandchildren. He received a Bachelor of Arts in Biblical Studies and his Doctor of Ministry from the Minnesota Graduate School of Theology. He is currently an Associate Pastor at Northview Christian Church, in Dothan, Alabama under the dynamic leadership of Pastor Hart Ramsey. Mr. Thornton's desire in life is to know Jesus more. It is in knowing Him that one discovers one's purpose for coming to earth. He is the author of the powerful book, *"When Have We Walked Together?"*

Men of My Father's Generation

www.ingramcontent.com/pod-product-compliance
Lightning Source LLC
Chambersburg PA
CBHW050557300426
44112CB00013B/1957